ANN NICOL

Glorious CAKES

ANN NICOL

Glorious

CAKES

CHARLES LETTS · *Letts* of London® · FOUNDED 1796

First published 1992
by Charles Letts & Co Ltd
Letts of London House
Parkgate Road
London SW11 4NQ

Reprinted 1993

Designed and edited by
Anness Publishing Limited
Boundary Row Studios
1–7 Boundary Row
London SE1 8HP

© 1992 Ann Nicol

Published in
Australia by
J.B. Fairfax Press
Pty Limited
by arrangement with
Charles Letts & Co Ltd,
London, United Kingdom.

ISBN 1 85238 196 5

A CIP catalogue record
for this book is available
from the British Library.

'Letts' is a registered
trademark of
Charles Letts
& Co. Ltd.

Editorial Director:
JOANNA LORENZ
Designer:
PETER BRIDGEWATER
Illustrations:
VANA HAGGERTY
Text Editor:
NORMA MCMILLAN
Project Editor:
JENNIFER JONES
Photographer:
KULBIR THANDI
Home Economist:
JACQUELINE CLARKE
Home Economist on Jacket:
STEVEN WHEELER

Printed and Bound in
Hong Kong
by Regent Publishing
Services Ltd.

To Bill, who has shared the last twenty years, and many, many cakes, with me.

$\mathscr{C}$ONTENTS

INTRODUCTION

*H*ome-made cakes are simply very special. They are signs of love and affection for family and friends, which no shop-bought cake, however luxurious, can duplicate. There is nothing quite like the unmistakable aroma of baking in a house, or the satisfaction gained from laying a tea table with home-made good things, or baking and giving your own cakes.

As technology advances, however, it seems that the tradition of baking is becoming more of a creative hobby, and not a weekly task. There are lots of 'weekend bakers', who, according to surveys, like to relieve the stress of a busy week by baking. I think this is a wonderful turnaround, as there can be no better way of relaxing than by beating butter, kneading dough, or whisking eggs to a froth. We all lead busy lives these days, and many people say they have no time to bake. I think it's always worth making the time, and I have in fact included some very quick bakes indeed.

This book is for both new and experienced bakers, and I have used a simple step-by-step approach to each recipe. I've tried to include cakes for every occasion, and have tips and hints to help when something goes wrong.

I've been hooked on making and decorating cakes ever since I was a child, so it has been a very enjoyable task to collect all my well-used and often food-splattered recipes together into one book for you to share. I do hope you will enjoy baking and eating them as much as I do.

ANN NICOL

C AKE BAKING:
THE BASICS

There are a few basic rules to observe before you start. Selecting the best ingredients and using appropriate equipment are important factors in ensuring the success of a recipe, and some guidelines are given here.

INGREDIENTS

EGGS

Eggs help raise the cake and provide richness. Use 4–5-day-old eggs, which have lost a little moisture, and stick to the size specified in the recipe if possible. Eggs should be used at room temperature to achieve the best aeration. Don't use cold eggs straight from the refrigerator, where they should be stored, but take them out to stand at room temperature for at least an hour before use. If you are in a hurry, put the eggs in a bowl, cover them with warm water and leave for 10 minutes to take off the chill.

It is a good idea to break the eggs one at a time into a teacup before beating them into the mixture, just in case one egg is not sound. This is also a good idea when you are separating a lot of egg whites and wish to keep out any specks of yolk and pieces of shell.

FATS

Fat gives a richer flavour to cakes, makes them tender and improves the keeping qualities. Butter and hard or block margarine are interchangeable, but butter gives the best flavour and should be used wherever possible. Soft tub margarine is only suitable for the all-in-one type recipe; if it is used for creaming, the mixture will become too wet. Always use fats at room temperature because this makes the job of creaming much easier and quicker.

Oil is sometimes called for in recipes, and mild-flavoured oils like vegetable or sunflower are best to use.

SUGAR

Sugar is not just for sweetness; it also makes the cake tender and soft and helps produce a spongy texture. Always use the type of sugar stated in the recipe.

CASTER SUGAR: this is the best white sugar for most baking as it creams easily with butter and dissolves easily and quickly into the mixture.

DEMERARA: this sugar is granular and mainly used for decorative purposes or for cake mixtures where the sugar is dissolved over heat.

SOFT LIGHT AND DARK BROWN SUGARS: these cream well, and are mostly used in fruit cake recipes, where rich flavour and colour are needed. Muscovado is the best soft dark brown sugar, as it is naturally unrefined and has an excellent rich flavour and dark colour.

GRANULATED: this is a coarser white sugar which is not really suitable for baking as it does not dissolve easily. It is used for frostings and boiled icings.

ICING SUGAR: this white sugar is very fine and powdery. It is used mainly for decoration, not baking. Keep it in a dry place and always sift before use as it tends to form lumps in storage.

FLOUR

PLAIN AND SELF-RAISING: flour provides the structure that makes the cake, so the right choice is vital. Self-raising flour is used for plain mixtures that contain no fruit, etc, and it has raising agents already mixed into it. Richer cakes that do not need raising agents are made with plain flour, or plain flour plus a small amount of a raising agent. If a recipe calls for self-raising flour and you have none, use 2½ tsp baking powder to each 225g/8oz plain flour.

STRONG PLAIN FLOUR: cakes baked with yeast need strong flour, as it enables the dough to stretch further. It gives a light open springy texture to the cake.

WHOLEWHEAT AND WHOLEMEAL FLOURS: these contain all the bran from the wheat and give good texture, flavour and fibre to cakes. Good in rich fruit cakes, you may need to add a little extra liquid, as the bran absorbs more of this.

These produce a light texture in cakes, and it is important to be very accurate when measuring them out.

BAKING POWDER: this is a ready-made mixture of bicarbonate of soda and cream of tartar. When liquid is added, the baking powder effervesces and produces carbon dioxide, and the heat of the oven expands these gas bubbles to give the cake an airy texture.

BICARBONATE OF SODA: this is a raising agent with a gentler effect. It is sometimes used to give heavy or spicy mixtures a lift. It must be measured accurately as too much bicarbonate of soda will give a bitter aftertaste.

CREAM OF TARTAR: this is a fast-acting raising agent: it begins to work the moment it is in touch with liquid. Always bake the mixture as soon as possible after adding cream of tartar or its effect will be reduced.

DRIED FRUITS

Dried vine fruits are usually bought pre-washed and cleaned, but you may well find large pieces of stalk in some packs, so it is worth picking them over. All dried fruits benefit from an initial soaking in water, orange juice, or an alcohol such as sherry, rum or brandy, to plump them up, but make sure to pat them dry in a tea towel or kitchen paper before use or they will sink in the cake mixture. Glacé and crystallized fruits like cherries should be washed in warm water to remove their syrup before use, or the sugary coating will dissolve on baking and drag the fruit down. Toss whole cherries in flour before baking to stop them from sinking.

CHOCOLATE

Always buy the very best chocolate for baking. Do not use the cheaper chocolate-flavoured cake covering as this is not true chocolate, and it has a high palm oil content which makes it melt at low temperatures. Choose the highest quality chocolate you can find, although this will probably be the most expensive.

$\mathcal{S}$ ECRETS OF SUCCESS

CAKE TINS

Always use the size of tin specified in the recipe, or the cakes will turn out peaked, cracked or sunk in the middle. Choose good quality, rigid tins that will last well. Jumble sale and charity shops are good places to pick up really strong, old cake tins that only need a good scrub.

PREPARING TINS: tins without a non-stick finish should be greased and lined before use; non-stick tins need only a light greasing. Apply a thin film of melted margarine using a pastry brush, or rub a margarine paper round the tin with your fingers.

Line deep tins round the base and sides. To do this, cut a piece of greaseproof or non-stick silicone paper big enough so that when folded double it will be about 5 cm/2 inches wider than the tin depth. Fold up the folded edge of the strip about 2.5 cm/1 inch and snip with scissors along the folded portion in a slanting direction. Grease the tin and line the sides with the strip, with the snipped edge on the bottom, lying flat. The lining should stand about 2.5 cm/1 inch higher than the rim of the tin. Place a round of paper on the base of the tin to cover the snipped edge. Greaseproof paper should be greased, but non-stick paper does not require this.

To line sandwich or shallow tins, place the tin on a sheet of greaseproof paper and trace round the tin with a pen. Cut out the shape, which will fit the base exactly, grease the paper and then put it in the tin.

Lining a round cake tin:

Cut non-stick paper into double-strip wider than tin depth. Make slanting cuts along top of strip, then place round inside edge

Cut a circle to fit base and insert

Lining a cornered tin:

Use tin as guide to cut paper piece, larger all round

Fold edges up around tin, then fit snugly inside

Brush paper lightly with oil or butter

TEMPERATURES AND OVENS

Always preheat the oven in good time before you start to bake, and arrange the shelves before placing the cake in the oven. Heavy and rich fruit cakes will need low temperatures, and take longer to cook. If the oven is too hot the outside will burn before the inside has had time to cook. Lighter mixtures need hotter temperatures and faster baking times.

The new types of fan-assisted ovens circulate hot air round the oven, and they heat up very quickly, so reduce the temperature by 10% of what the recipe states. You may even need to reduce the cooking time. Get to know your oven and follow the manufacturer's instructions.

ℋOW TO TELL
WHEN A CAKE IS COOKED

☞ The centre of a cake is the very last part to bake, so cook for the time directed, then test the centre. For a sponge mixture, do this by pressing lightly with a fingertip: the cake should only give very slightly. If it feels springy, and no imprint remains, the cake is done. It should also have shrunk a little from the sides of the tin.

☞ Small cakes should be well risen, golden and just firm to the touch when pressed lightly.

☞ Lift large fruit cakes from the oven and listen to them! If the cake is not fully cooked, there will still be a bubbling or sizzling noise in the centre.

☞ To test creamed or fruit cakes, insert a very thin warmed metal skewer into the deepest part; it will come out perfectly clean if the cake is cooked. (To warm a skewer easily for testing, place it between the tin and the paper lining for a few seconds.)

Test creamed and fruit cakes
by inserting a skewer

𝒞OOLING CAKES

☞ All freshly baked cakes are very fragile whilst still warm, so leave them in the tin for at least 3 minutes before turning them out.

☞ Rich fruit cakes are very pliable when newly cooked, so leave these in the tin for longer. Very rich fruit cakes, like wedding cakes, should be left in the tin until completely cold.

☞ Loosen sponge cakes from the sides of the tin with a palette knife, then turn on to a wire rack. Immediately flip over on to another wire rack to prevent the top of the cake from being marked with a criss-cross pattern.

☞ Set delicate sponges, still in their tins, on a damp tea towel for a few minutes before turning out, and they will slip out more easily.

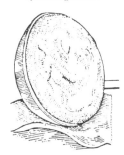

Leave cakes in tin for
3 minutes before turning out

Turn sponge cakes on to
a wire rack .
Flip on to another rack
to avoid marking the top

Storing and Freezing Cakes

☞ Be sure the cake is completely cold before storing it in an airtight tin. If the cake is not completely cold, condensation will form in the tin, which could cause mould.

☞ Keep cakes with fresh cream fillings and icings in the refrigerator.

☞ Store cakes and biscuits separately, or the biscuits will go soggy.

☞ If you do not have a large airtight tin, invert a Pyrex bowl over the cake, being sure the bowl rests flat on the cake plate or work surface, and it will keep just as fresh.

☞ Store un-iced rich fruit cakes in their baking papers. Prick the surface of the cake and brush with a little brandy, then overwrap in clean greaseproof paper and seal with sticky tape. Overwrap again in a double layer of foil, and tape up tightly. Before icing and decorating wedding and Christmas cakes, keep them in storage for 6 weeks minimum, ideally 4 months, to mellow the flavour and produce a really rich moist texture.

☞ Fatless sponges will keep for 1–2 days only; Genoese sponges, 3 days; Victoria or creamed sponges, up to 1 week. Light fruit cakes will store in a tin for 2–2½ weeks, and rich fruit cakes a month or much longer if not cut.

☞ Each recipe gives freezer notes, but most undecorated cakes will freeze well. Overwrap in freezer film or bags or foil, trying to exclude as much air as possible. Unwrap before thawing, and allow plenty of time to thaw at room temperature.

$\mathcal{G}$UIDE TO
BETTER BAKING

$\mathcal{T}$here are various methods of baking. These are the main ones used in this book:

THE CREAMING METHOD

This is used for sponge and fruit cakes where the amount of fat is equal to all, or half, the weight of the flour. The key to success is lengthy beating of the fat with sugar to form a fluffy, light foundation into which the whole eggs or egg whites can be lightly beaten. Heavier ingredients, such as flour, nuts or dried fruits, are lightly folded into the creamed mixture. When adding the eggs, break them into a bowl and beat with a fork, then add to the creamed mixture slowly. If they are added too quickly, or they are too cold, the mixture will curdle. Adding a little flour with each addition of egg will help prevent the mixture separating at this stage.

THE WHISKING METHOD

This is used for light sponge-type cakes such as Genoese and angel cakes. Eggs are whisked with sugar until a thick ribbon will form when the whisk is lifted away. Flour and melted fat or oil are gently folded into the thick foamy mixture, which must be baked immediately or the air beaten in will be lost. To produce a good volume of air in the mixture, it must be warm. Place the mixing bowl over a pan or bowl of hot water, or gently heat the bowl and sugar first if using a table-top mixer. To achieve a golden crust, dust the cake tins after greasing with half flour and half caster sugar.

ALL-IN-ONE METHOD

Cakes made by this method are so quickly mixed, it is important not to start before you have heated the oven properly. All the ingredients are placed in one bowl and quickly beaten together. Soft tub margarines are the best fat to use in these cakes, and extra raising agent, usually baking powder, is needed, even if self-raising flour is used. Do not leave the mixture to stand before baking as the raising agent will start to work immediately.

RIGHT (from top to bottom): Rich Fruit Cake (see page 96), decorated with fondant icing (see page 164) and flowers (see page 179); Twelfth Night Cake (see page 99); Chocolate Yule Log, or *Bûche de Noël* (see page 50).

This is used for cakes like gingerbread and honey cake. The fat and sugar, treacle or honey are gently heated together until melted, then cooled and beaten into the dry ingredients. The mixture must be beaten well with a wooden spoon at this stage, to develop the gluten in the flour. A raising agent and, usually, an egg are needed to add lightness. Because of their high sugar content, these cakes take longer to bake. It is imperative not to open the oven door for at least the first 45 minutes of baking, or the cake will collapse. Melted cakes are quick and easy to make and ideal for introducing children to baking.

O V E N T E M P E R A T U R E C H A R T			
°C	**°F**	**Gas Mark**	**Temperature**
110	225	¼	Very cool
130	250	½	Very cool
140	275	1	Very cool
150	300	2	Cool
160/170	325	3	Warm
180	350	4	Moderate
190	375	5	Fairly hot
200	400	6	Fairly hot
210/220	425	7	Hot
230	450	8	Very hot
240	475	9	Very hot

NOTES ON CONVERSIONS

The recipes in this book give ingredients in metric and imperial measures. It is important to follow only one set of measures, and never to mix them, as they are not exact equivalents.

The table below shows the equivalents used in this book.

25g	1oz
50g	2oz
75g	3oz
100g	4oz
150g	5oz
175g	6oz
200g	7oz
225g	8oz
250g	9oz
275g	10oz
300g	11oz
325/350g	12oz
375g	13oz
400g	14oz
425g	15oz
450g	16oz (1lb)
675g	1½lb
900g	2lb
1kg	2¼lb

All spoon measures are level unless otherwise noted. Spoon measures used are based on metric spoons: 1 tablespoon = 15ml, 1 teaspoon = 5ml.

LEFT (from top to bottom): Mocha Nut Squares (see page 89); Baklava (see page 87); Easy Cupcakes and Butterflies (see page 82).

SPONGE AND LIGHT CAKES

CHAPTER ONE

The key to making successful cakes by the creaming method is thorough beating of the fat and sugar, to give the cake a good base and to incorporate as much air as possible. Start by using butter or block margarine at room temperature or soft tub margarine, which are easier to cream. Use a balloon whisk, wooden spoon or electric mixer and beat vigorously until the mixture becomes pale and fluffy, and almost doubles in bulk. When well creamed, most mixtures will be very pale in colour, and soft and floppy in texture. It is then easy to incorporate the eggs, or egg yolks. Beat these in one at a time to prevent curdling the mixture, then fold in flour or nuts with a large metal spoon using a figure-of-eight motion, trying to keep in as much air as possible.

Cakes produced by the whisked or Genoese method have a lovely light texture, but do need skill to prepare. For the Genoese method, whole eggs and sugar are whisked together until a trail or ribbon forms when the whisk is lifted. The whisking is done in a bowl set over hot water to help thicken the mixture, and the use of an electric mixer really helps, as this mixture needs beating for a long time until the correct consistency is achieved.

CLASSIC VICTORIA SANDWICH

This cake was made in the time of Queen Victoria, when only butter was used. Butter does give a rich colour and flavour to a plain cake, so do use it if you can. The secret of a sponge cake is in the creaming so always ensure the butter and sugar mixture is really light and fluffy. I learnt this by experience when I had to make 200 Victorias for a TV flour commercial!

- 175 G/6 OZ BUTTER OR BLOCK MARGARINE, AT ROOM TEMPERATURE
- 175 G/6 OZ CASTER SUGAR
- 3 EGGS, SIZE 3, AT ROOM TEMPERATURE, BEATEN
- 175 G/6 OZ SELF-RAISING FLOUR, SIFTED
- FEW DROPS VANILLA ESSENCE, OR ½ TSP GRATED LEMON ZEST
- ICING SUGAR, TO DREDGE

FILLING:
- 4–5 TBSP RASPBERRY JAM
- 150 ML/¼ PINT WHIPPING CREAM, WHIPPED

1 Set the oven to 180°C/350°F/Gas 4. Grease and base-line two 20cm/8inch round sandwich tins.

2 Put the butter or margarine in a bowl and beat until very soft, using an electric mixer if possible. Add the sugar and beat together until the mixture is light, fluffy and pale in colour.

3 Beat in the eggs, a little at a time, adding a teaspoon of the flour with each addition to prevent the mixture from curdling. Gently fold in the remaining flour with the essence or zest and 1 tbsp water.

4 Divide the mixture between the tins and spread level. Bake in the centre of the oven for about 30 minutes or until well risen, light golden and firm to the touch. Leave to cool in the tins for at least 3 minutes, then turn out on to wire racks to cool completely. Peel away the lining paper when cold.

5 Place the base of one cake on your prettiest serving plate and spread with raspberry jam; cover the underside of the other with whipped cream and sandwich together. Sprinkle with sifted icing sugar and serve immediately.

TO FREEZE: *Wrap unfilled sponges in foil. Keeps for 3 months.*

Illustrated opposite page 33

Genoese Sponge

*This is a very light sponge that keeps well, providing a good base for
a decorated special occasion cake. Add the butter very gradually in
a slow thin trickle to avoid making the cake heavy.*

- 3 EGGS, SIZE 2
- 75 G/3 OZ CASTER SUGAR,
  STORED WITH A VANILLA POD
- 65 G/2½ OZ PLAIN FLOUR
- 1 TBSP CORNFLOUR

- 40 G/1½ OZ BUTTER,
  MELTED AND COOLED
- FILLING AND TOPPING
  (SEE STEP 7)

1 Set the oven to 180°C/350°F/Gas 4. Grease and base-line two 18cm/7inch sandwich tins or one 20cm/8inch round deep cake tin.

2 Place the eggs and sugar in a heatproof bowl and set over a large saucepan of hot water. Whisk until very thick and pale, and firm enough to leave a ribbon trail when the whisk is lifted. This will take about 6–7 minutes using an electric mixer at medium speed. Remove from the hot water and continue whisking until cool.

3 Sift the flour and cornflour together. Gradually fold half into the whisked mixture using a large metal spoon.

4 Gradually fold in the melted butter alternately with the remaining flour mixture, using as light a touch as possible or the butter will sink and the cake will be heavy.

5 Pour into the tin(s) and bake above the centre of the oven for about 25 minutes for the sandwich tins and 35–40 minutes for the deep cake tin. The cakes should be well risen, firm to the touch and just beginning to shrink away from the sides of the tin.

6 Leave to cool in the tin for about 3 minutes, then turn out on to a wire rack to cool completely. Peel away the lining paper when cold.

7 Cut the larger cake into two or three horizontal layers. Sandwich with filling and decorate (see Icings and Fillings, pages 156–71, and Cake Decoration, pages 172–87).

TO FREEZE: *Wrap unfilled cake in foil. Keeps for up to 2 months.*

$\mathcal{A}$LL-IN-ONE
SPONGE CAKE

This is the easiest and quickest sponge cake to make. As the cake is not beaten for long, you need to add baking powder for extra lightness. The cake freezes well, retaining all its moisture.

- 175 G/6 OZ SELF-RAISING FLOUR
- 1 TSP BAKING POWDER
- 175 G/6 OZ CASTER SUGAR

- 175 G/6 OZ SOFT TUB MARGARINE
- FEW DROPS VANILLA ESSENCE
- 3 EGGS, SIZE 3, BEATEN

1 Grease and base-line the tin of required size (see chart below). Set the oven to 180°C/350°F/Gas 4.

2 Sift the flour and baking powder into a bowl, then add all the remaining ingredients.

3 Beat together with a wooden spoon quickly until combined. Do not overbeat or the mixture will become wet. Add the chosen flavouring variation if required (see opposite).

4 Spread the mixture in the tin and bake according to the chart below or until the sponge is light golden and springy to the touch. Leave to cool in tin for about 3 minutes, then run a knife round the inside of the tin and turn the cake on to a wire rack to cool completely. Decorate when cold.

TIN SIZES & COOKING TIMES

20cm/8inch round deep tin: 50 minutes – 1 hour

two 18cm/7inch sandwich tins: 30 minutes

15cm/6inch square deep tin: 50 minutes

20cm/8in ring mould: 40 minutes

900g/2lb loaf tin: 50 minutes

23cm/9in shallow slab tin: 40 minutes

TO FREEZE: *Wrap undecorated in freezer bags or foil. Keeps for 3 months.*

QUICK VARIATIONS FOR ALL-IN-ONE SPONGE CAKES

CHOCOLATE CHIP

Fold 100g/4oz small chocolate drops into the basic mixture.

LEMON

Stir the grated zest of 2 lemons and 1 tbsp lemon juice into the basic mixture.

ORANGE

Stir the finely grated zest of 2 oranges and the chopped, seeded flesh of 1 orange into the basic mixture.

GINGER

Finely chop 3 pieces of preserved stem ginger in syrup and add to the basic mixture.

CHERRY

Wash, drain and chop 100g/4oz glacé cherries and fold into the basic mixture with 25g/1oz ground almonds.

WALNUT

Fold 75g/3oz chopped walnuts into the basic mixture.

BUTTERSCOTCH

Use only 100g/4oz caster sugar to make the basic mixture. Melt 75g/3oz cream toffees with 1 tbsp golden syrup in a small pan or in the microwave oven. Leave to cool, then add to the mixture.

MOCHA

Replace 2 tbsp flour with cocoa powder. Dissolve 1 tbsp instant coffee powder in 2 tbsp boiling water and cool, then add to the mixture.

MARBLED CHOCOLATE AND ORANGE

Divide the basic mixture in half. To one half add 1 tbsp cocoa powder dissolved in 1 tbsp boiling water and cooled. To the other half add 1 tbsp orange juice and 1 tsp finely grated orange zest. Place alternate tablespoons of the mixture in the tin, then draw the spoon through the mixture, swirling it as you go to create a marbled pattern.

*L*EMON MADEIRA CAKE

*This classic cake keeps well for up to a week in an airtight tin, and
provides a good base for novelty cakes as it cuts firmly. Originally it
was decorated with a strip of citron peel on top, but this is very
difficult to obtain these days.*

* 175 G/6 OZ BUTTER,
AT ROOM TEMPERATURE
* 175 G/6 OZ CASTER SUGAR
* 3 EGGS, SIZE 3, BEATEN
* 175 G/6 OZ SELF-RAISING FLOUR
* 75 G/3 OZ PLAIN FLOUR

* FINELY GRATED ZEST
OF 1 LEMON
* 1 TBSP LEMON JUICE
* 1 THIN SLICE CITRON PEEL
(OPTIONAL)

1 Grease and base-line a 20cm/8inch round deep cake tin. Set the oven to
170°C/325°F/Gas 3.

2 Beat the butter and sugar together until light, fluffy and pale in colour. Gradually
add the eggs, beating well after each addition. Add a teaspoon of flour if the mixture
begins to curdle.

3 Sift the flours together, then fold into the mixture with the lemon zest and juice.

4 Spoon into the tin and level the top. If using the citron peel, place in the centre.
Bake in the centre of the oven for about 1 hour and 10 minutes or until firm to the
touch. Leave to cool in the tin for 10 minutes, then turn out on to a wire rack to cool
completely. Peel away the lining paper when cool.

*O*LD ENGLISH SEED CAKE

*This is a variation of Madeira cake which has been baked here
for over 300 years. It was always served with a glass of sweet wine
for morning refreshment in Victorian times. What a shame the
habit has died out.*

Follow the Madeira cake recipe above, omitting the lemon zest, juice and citron peel.
Add the following with the flours: 1 TBSP GROUND ALMONDS, 1 TBSP CARAWAY SEEDS
AND 2 TBSP MILK.

TO FREEZE: *Freeze the cake whole or in slices, wrapped in freezer bags. Keeps for up to
3 months.*

TIP: *Any leftover stale pieces of Madeira cake are excellent used in trifles. Sprinkle with a
little sherry before use.*

Illustrated opposite page 32

$\mathcal{A}$NGEL CAKE

If you ever have a surfeit of egg whites and are wondering what to do with them, make an angel cake. It is fatless, delicate and totally delicious. You really do need a large tube or ring cake tin, however, as if the angel cake is baked in an ordinary tin, the outside will dry out before the middle sets.

- 75 G/3 OZ PLAIN FLOUR
- 50 G/2 OZ CORNFLOUR
- 100 G/4 OZ ICING SUGAR
- 1 TSP CREAM OF TARTAR
- FEW DROPS VANILLA ESSENCE
- FEW DROPS ALMOND ESSENCE
- 10 EGG WHITES, SIZE 3
- 175 G/6 OZ CASTER SUGAR
- TOPPING (SEE STEP 6)

Turn cake out by inverting tin over a funnel

1 Set the oven to 190°C/375°F/Gas 5. Have ready an ungreased 25cm/10inch tubular or ring cake tin.

2 Sift the flour, cornflour and icing sugar together.

3 Take a large bowl and scald it with boiling water to ensure it is completely grease-free. Dry thoroughly, then add the cream of tartar, essences and egg whites. Whisk, preferably with an electric mixer, until the egg whites form soft peaks. Whisk in the caster sugar, a little at a time, and continue whisking until the mixture forms stiff peaks.

4 Fold in the flour mixture one-quarter at a time. Be careful not to overmix. Spoon into the ungreased tin, trying to ensure there are no large air bubbles.

5 Bake in the centre of the oven for about 45 minutes or until the cake lightly springs when touched with a fingertip. Remove from the oven and invert the tin on a wire rack over a funnel. Leave to cool upside-down in the tin, until completely cold.

6 Gently run a palette knife round the sides of the tin to release the cake, then turn out on to a serving plate. Serve the cake plain, or covered with seven-minute frosting (see page 166) or Italian meringue (see page 168), decorated with a thinly sliced lime and served with a sharp fresh raspberry sauce.

Not suitable for freezing.

Illustrated opposite page 128

*Pour caramel on to cake
and smooth over*

Mark cake into eight sections

DOBOS TORTE

*This gâteau is named after its creator, Dobos, a famous Hungarian
pâtissier from Budapest. It makes a really spectacular centrepiece
for a party.*

5 EGGS, SIZE 3
175 G/6 OZ CASTER SUGAR
150 G/5 OZ PLAIN FLOUR
50 G/2 OZ SHELLED HAZELNUTS,
CHOPPED AND TOASTED,
TO DECORATE
CARAMEL GLAZE:
150 G/5 OZ CASTER SUGAR

CHOCOLATE CREAM:
100 G/4 OZ DARK PLAIN
CHOCOLATE
225 G/8 OZ UNSALTED BUTTER,
AT ROOM TEMPERATURE
3 EGG WHITES, SIZE 3
150 G/5 OZ ICING SUGAR,
SIFTED

1 Take six sheets of non-stick silicone paper, each large enough to line a baking
sheet. Draw a 20cm/8inch circle on each sheet of paper. (An easy way to do this is to
trace round a saucepan lid.) Line one or more baking sheets with paper. Set the oven
to 200°C/400°F/Gas 6.

2 Place the eggs and sugar in a heatproof bowl and set this over a large saucepan of
hot water. Whisk until very thick and pale, and firm enough to leave a ribbon trail
when the whisk is lifted. Remove from the heat and continue whisking until cool.

3 Sift one-third of the flour over the mixture and fold it in, then continue with the
remaining flour in the same way.

4 Carefully spread one-sixth of the mixture on to each lined baking sheet inside the
drawn circle, making a neat round. Bake for 6–8 minutes until golden brown. Loosen
from the sheets and trim any edges while still warm, then leave to cool on the paper
on wire racks. Re-line the baking sheets, and bake six layers in total.

5 Take the round with the best and flattest surface and place it on an oiled baking
sheet. Put the caster sugar into a small, heavy-based saucepan and heat gently,
without stirring, until it melts and turns a light brown. Immediately pour the caramel
over the cake round on the baking sheet, spreading it out with an oiled palette knife.
Mark into eight sections, then trim the edges. Leave to cool and set.

6 To make the chocolate cream, place the chocolate in a small heatproof bowl and
set over a pan of warm water, until the chocolate has melted. Set aside to cool slightly.
Beat the butter until pale and fluffy, then beat in the chocolate until well combined.

7 Place the egg whites and icing sugar in a heatproof bowl set over a pan of hot
water and whisk until thick. Stir 2 tbsp into the chocolate mixture to soften it, then
fold in the remainder.

Illustrated opposite page 33

8 Fill a small piping bag fitted with a star nozzle with a few tablespoons of the chocolate cream. Sandwich the cake rounds together with two-thirds of the remaining chocolate cream, using the caramel-glazed cake for the top. Spread the sides of the cake with the remaining chocolate cream, then press the chopped nuts neatly on to the sides.

9 Pipe the chocolate cream into a neat star border all around the top of the cake between the caramel and the hazelnuts.

Not suitable for freezing.

$\mathcal{A}$LL-IN-ONE BIRTHDAY SPONGE

I call this a birthday sponge because I've been called on to make so many cakes at the last minute, and you can mix this one up in a trice. The evaporated milk helps keep it moist, so you can bake it the day before, or freeze it and ice it later when you have more time.

- 100 G/4 OZ SOFT TUB MARGARINE
- 100 G/4 OZ CASTER SUGAR
- 170 G/6 OZ SELF-RAISING FLOUR
- 2 EGGS, SIZE 3, BEATEN
- 3 TBSP EVAPORATED MILK
- ½ TSP VANILLA ESSENCE, OR FINELY GRATED ZEST OF ½ LEMON
- FILLING AND TOPPING (SEE STEP 5)

1 Set the oven to 190°C/375°F/Gas 5. Grease and line a 20cm/8inch round deep cake tin.

2 Place all the ingredients in a large bowl and beat with an electric mixer for 2 minutes, or for 3–4 minutes by hand, until smooth and creamy.

3 Spoon into the tin and spread level. Bake for about 45 minutes or until firm to the touch in the centre and pale golden.

4 Leave to cool in the tin for 5 minutes, then turn out on to a wire rack and peel away the lining paper.

5 When cold, split and fill with cream or jam, and cover with buttercream, frosting or fondant icing (see pages 170, 166 or 164).

TO FREEZE: *Wrap unfilled cake in foil. Keeps for 3 months.*

TIPSY CAKE

This cake doubles up as a wonderful pudding. You could cheat and make it with bought sponge cakes, but the home-made ones really taste best.

GENOESE SPONGE CAKE
(SEE PAGE 23), BAKED IN TWO
18 CM/7 INCH SANDWICH TINS
4 TBSP APRICOT GLAZE
(SEE PAGE 169)
25 G/ 1OZ AMARETTI BISCUITS,
ROUGHLY CRUSHED
25 G/ 1OZ PLAIN CHOCOLATE,
COARSELY GRATED
25 G/ 1OZ FLAKED ALMONDS

4 TBSP GOLDEN SYRUP
2 TBSP AMARETTO OR OTHER
ALMOND LIQUEUR
2 TBSP TIA MARIA, KALUHA
OR OTHER COFFEE LIQUEUR
300 ML/½ PINT WHIPPING
CREAM, SOFTLY WHIPPED OR
1 QUANTITY SEVEN-MINUTE
FROSTING (SEE PAGE 166)

1 Split the two sponge cakes in half horizontally, and spread the bottom layer of each with apricot glaze. Roughly chop the other 2 layers into large pieces. Divide the pieces into three portions. Mix the amaretti biscuits into one portion, the chocolate into another portion, and the flaked almonds into the third.

2 Gently warm the golden syrup in two separate bowls set in a pan of hot water. Add the almond liqueur to one and the coffee liqueur to the other. When the syrup is liquid, pour the almond syrup over the cake and almond mixture and stir; pour the coffee syrup over the chocolate and cake mixture and stir.

3 Place one glaze-covered cake layer on a serving plate. Cover with the soaked and plain cake pieces alternately and pat together neatly, then place the other jam-covered layer on top, glaze side down. Press together, then chill for 4 hours to firm the cake.

4 Cover the cake with cream or seven-minute frosting, swirled roughly round the top and sides. Decorate with fondant, frosted or real flowers (see pages 179–81 or 185) to serve.

Not suitable for freezing.

Illustrated opposite page 32

ℬATTENBERG CAKE

This sponge cake, made from coloured squares, makes a popular addition to the tea table. It originated in Germany, when Prince Henry of Battenberg married Beatrice, one of Queen Victoria's daughters (the name changed later to Mountbatten).

- 100 G/4 OZ BUTTER, AT ROOM TEMPERATURE
- 100 G/4 OZ CASTER SUGAR
- 2 EGGS, SIZE 3, BEATEN
- FEW DROPS ALMOND ESSENCE
- 100 G/4 OZ SELF-RAISING FLOUR, SIFTED
- PINK FOOD COLOURING

TO FINISH:
- 3 TBSP RASPBERRY JAM
- 4 TBSP APRICOT GLAZE (SEE PAGE 169)
- 225 G/8 OZ ALMOND PASTE (SEE PAGE 160)

1 Set the oven to 180°C/350°F/Gas 4. Grease and base-line an 18cm/7inch square cake tin.

2 Beat the butter and sugar together until light, fluffy and pale in colour. Add the eggs gradually, beating well after each addition. Add the almond essence, then gradually fold in the flour with a metal spoon. Divide the mixture in half and colour one half pink with the food colouring.

3 Spoon the plain mixture in one half of the tin, divide with a strip of foil, making a neat line in the middle, then spoon the pink mixture on the other side. Smooth the top level, then bake in the centre of the oven for 30–35 minutes or until firm to the touch in the middle. Cool in the tin for 3 minutes, then turn out of the tin, remove the lining paper and leave to cool.

4 Divide the cake down the middle into a pink half and a white half, then cut each half in half lengthways to form four oblongs. Brush two long sides of each piece with raspberry jam and stack them on top of each other to form a chequerboard pattern.

5 Brush the four long sides of the cake with apricot glaze, leaving the ends free. Roll out the almond paste into a rectangle to fit the length of the cake and four times the width of one side. Place the cake on the almond paste and press it round to cover all the sides. Make a fluted ridge on the top edges by pinching the paste between your thumb and forefinger. Score a diamond pattern on the top with a sharp knife.

TO FREEZE: *Wrap finished cake in foil. Keeps for 3 months.*

Illustrated opposite page 33

Cut both cake colours into four oblongs

Stack alternate colours, securing with jam

Roll almond paste into a rectangle and wrap over

Pinch paste on top edges to flute

Spread sponge base

with warmed jam

Roll up from the short end

When rolled, cool on

a wire rack

RIGHT (from top to
bottom): Tipsy Cake
(see page 30); Old
English Seed Cake (see
page 26); Swiss Roll
(see above).

$\mathcal{S}$WISS ROLL

A Swiss roll can double up as a useful pudding, served with cream
or fromage frais and fresh fruit. It can also be made ahead and
filled just before serving.

- 3 EGGS, SIZE 2
- 100 G/4 OZ CASTER SUGAR
- 100 G/4 OZ PLAIN FLOUR

- 6 TBSP WARMED JAM
- ICING SUGAR, TO DREDGE

1 Brush a 33 × 23cm/13 × 9inch Swiss roll tin with melted margarine. Cut a piece of greaseproof paper 5cm/2inches larger than the tin all round. Place in the tin, snipping the corners to fit, then brush the paper with melted margarine. Set the oven to 200°C/400°F/Gas 6.

2 Place the eggs and caster sugar in a heatproof bowl and set over a saucepan of hot water. Whisk, using an electric mixer if possible, until very thick and pale, and firm enough to leave a ribbon trail when the whisk is lifted. Remove from the heat and continue whisking until cold.

3 Sift half the flour into the mixture and fold in with a large metal spoon. Fold in 1 tbsp warm water and then the rest of the flour.

4 Pour into the prepared tin, spreading the mixture evenly into all the corners. Bake for 7–10 minutes until golden and firm to the touch.

5 While the cake is baking, make preparations for turning it out: wring out a clean tea towel in hot water and spread it out on a work surface. Spread a sheet of greaseproof paper on top of this and sprinkle with caster sugar.

6 Turn the cooked cake out of the tin directly on to the sugared paper. Working quickly, while the cake is still hot, peel off the lining paper and trim away the crusty edges. Spread with the warmed jam to within 1cm/½inch of the edges.

7 Roll up from a short side, using the paper to help guide you. When completely rolled up, leave covered in the paper to stop the cake from unrolling. To serve, remove the paper, sift icing sugar lightly over and slice.

How to fill with cream instead of jam:
Roll up as above, but without the jam and rolling the sugared paper inside, to prevent the cake sticking to itself. Leave to cool completely. When cold, unroll very carefully, trying to avoid cracking the cake, and remove the paper. Spread with ¼ pint/150 ml whipped cream, or cream and small pieces of fruit, and roll up again carefully.

TO FREEZE: *Wrap unfilled cake in foil. Keeps for 3 months.*

Illustrated opposite page 32

WHAT WENT WRONG?

☞ THE CAKE HAS A DOMED TOP:
This happens if the mixture is not creamed enough, or the cake was baked in too hot an oven or on too high a shelf in the oven.

☞ THE SPONGE HAS A CLOSE, DOUGHY TEXTURE:
This happens if you add too much egg, fat or flour, or too little raising agent. Inadequate creaming or beating or underbaking can also cause this.

☞ SPECKLES ON TOP OF THE CAKE:
Insufficient creaming could cause this, because the sugar remains undissolved before baking; or insufficient sifting of ingredients together.

☞ A CRUSTY RING FORMS ROUND THE SIDES:
Over-greasing the tins can cause this.

☞ HOLES OR TUNNELS FORM IN THE CENTRE OR THE TEXTURE IS UNEVEN:
This can be caused by overmixing or uneven mixing when folding in flour. A mixture that is too dry can trap pockets of air and this will also happen if the raising agent and flour are not properly sifted together.

☞ WHISKED SPONGE IS VERY SHALLOW AND DOES NOT RISE:
This happens if the mixture is not whisked sufficiently, or it is baked in too cool an oven.

☞ THE TOP SINKS IN THE MIDDLE:
This can happen if the mixture contained too much raising agent, the fat and sugar were overcreamed, or soft tub margarine was used (only use this for quick all-in-one mixes). Using too cool an oven or opening and slamming the door during baking can also cause this.

☞ SWISS ROLL IS THIN AND BADLY RISEN:
The mixture did not contain enough air, due to insufficient whisking.

☞ SWISS ROLL CRACKED WHEN ROLLED:
The cake was not rolled quickly enough before cooling, or the crusty edges were not trimmed off.

LEFT (from top to bottom): Dobos Torte (see page 28); Classic Victoria Sandwich (see page 22); Battenberg Cake (see page 31).

CHOCOLATE CAKES

CHAPTER TWO

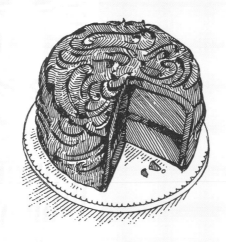

*C*hocolate came to us from the New World in the 16th century, and the craze for it has never left us. Smooth and rich in texture and flavour, chocolate is loved by almost everyone, including the gods – its Greek name theobroma cacao *means 'food of the gods'. It was considered as great a luxury as gold by the Aztecs and was served to the men only at the court of Montezuma. Female members were forbidden it, possibly because of its reputed aphrodisiac powers! It still has very romantic connotations today, as is seen by the popularity of chocolate cakes and chocolates on Valentine's Day.*

The flavour of chocolate blends beautifully with many spices, fruits, liqueurs and cream to form the most decadent of luxuries – chocolate cake! Served for morning coffee, lunch, tea or as a pudding, eaten day or night, it is the most self-indulgent treat ever.

CHOCOLATE
CAKES

Melt chocolate in a
double saucepan

WORKING WITH
CHOCOLATE AND COCOA

Chocolate needs to be pampered and treated with respect; if not, it will show its prima donna-like qualities and become temperamental and obstinate and refuse to co-operate. Be gentle with it and it will comply with your every wish.

FOLLOW THESE RULES FOR SUCCESS:

☞ Always buy the most expensive chocolate available. Price is a good indication of quality and the flavour of real chocolate far outweighs the economic gains of the cheaper varieties, which may not contain real cocoa fat.

☞ Store chocolate and cocoa in a cool, dark place. Wrap opened chocolate tightly in foil, and it will keep almost indefinitely. Use cocoa powder within a year as it tends to taste musty after this.

☞ To melt chocolate successfully, place the broken pieces in the top of a double boiler over warm but not hot water. If you do not have a double boiler, put the chocolate in a small heatproof bowl over a pan of warm water. Make sure the pan or bowl containing the chocolate is completely dry – water and steam are the enemy while the chocolate is melting (you can, however, melt chocolate with milk, butter or water as long as these are added to the pan with the chocolate – see below). Also make sure the base of the pan or bowl does not actually touch the water. Heat very gently, melting without stirring, for about 10 minutes. If the chocolate reaches a temperature higher than blood heat, it will lose its sheen on cooling.

☞ If the chocolate gets too hot and starts to stiffen, stir in a little vegetable margarine – not butter.

☞ If chocolate comes into contact with water or steam it becomes a thick rough mass that will refuse to melt. This can be corrected by stirring in a little vegetable oil or margarine, 1 teaspoon at a time, until the mixture becomes smooth again. This is an emergency measure though, and may alter the final balance of the recipe.

☞ Combine the melted chocolate with other ingredients while it is warm and easy to pour. Try to keep other liquids at the same temperature, as a liquid hotter than the chocolate, or ice cold, will cause the cocoa butter to separate and make the chocolate lumpy.

☞ If chocolate is melted together with milk, butter or water, the process can be done directly over a gentle heat in a heavy-based pan, but you will need to stir and watch it all the time.

☞ White chocolate is the most difficult to work with. It helps to grate it finely first, and keep the heat very low when melting. If white chocolate starts to 'tighten', add a few drops of boiling water to smooth it.

☞ Cocoa grains need to be cooked for the full flavour to emerge, so blend to a paste with boiling water before adding to a cake mixture.

☞ Don't substitute drinking chocolate for cocoa powder, as this contains sugar and milk powder and will spoil the flavour of a cake.

☞ Chocolate can be successfully melted in a bowl in the microwave oven. Use short bursts of power to avoid over-cooking, depending on the amount of chocolate being used.

Sachertorte

This is one of the world's most popular chocolate cakes and should be served simply, covered in chocolate icing, with the word 'Sacher' piped across. Use only the finest quality dark chocolate for this cake.

- 150 G/5 OZ PLAIN CHOCOLATE
- 150 G/5 OZ UNSALTED BUTTER, AT ROOM TEMPERATURE
- 150 G/5 OZ CASTER SUGAR, STORED WITH A VANILLA POD
- 6 EGGS, SIZE 2, SEPARATED
- 150 G/5 OZ PLAIN FLOUR, SIFTED

- 6 TBSP APRICOT GLAZE (SEE PAGE 169)
- 50 G/2 OZ MILK CHOCOLATE
- **CHOCOLATE ICING:**
- 175 G/6 OZ PLAIN CHOCOLATE
- 4 TBSP BLACK COFFEE
- 175 G/6 OZ ICING SUGAR

1 Grease, base-line and flour a loose-based 20cm/8inch round deep cake tin. Set the oven to 180°C/350°F/Gas 4.

2 Break up the chocolate and melt it gently in a heatproof bowl set over a pan of warm water, or in the microwave oven. Cool slightly. Beat the butter with half the sugar until light, fluffy and pale in colour. Beat in the melted chocolate, then the egg yolks, one at a time.

Cut cake horizontally in half

3 Whisk the egg whites until stiff, then fold them gently into the mixture with the flour and remaining sugar. Spoon into the prepared tin and level the top. Bake for about 1¼ hours or until a skewer inserted into the middle comes out clean. Leave to cool in the tin for 10 minutes, then turn out on to a wire rack to cool completely.

4 If the cake has domed, slice a thin layer off the top to level it. Cut the cake horizontally in half. Heat the glaze and use 2 tablespoons to sandwich the layers together. Spread the rest of the glaze over the top and sides of the cake.

Sandwich layers together with warm glaze

5 To make the icing, melt the chocolate with the coffee in a small heatproof bowl set over a pan of warm water. Gradually sift in the icing sugar, beating well. Working very quickly, spread the icing over the top and down the sides of the cake, using a large palette knife. The icing will thicken as it sets, so make sure all bare patches are covered and smooth. Place the cake on a serving plate and leave the icing to set for about 2 hours.

6 For the icing melt the milk chocolate in a small heatproof bowl set over a pan of warm water, then place in a greaseproof paper piping bag (see page 182). Snip off the end, then pipe the word 'Sacher' on top of the cake. Leave to set for 30 minutes.

Spread chocolate icing over glaze with a palette knife

TO FREEZE: *Open-freeze decorated or undecorated, then store in a rigid container. Keeps for 3 months. Thaw for 4 hours before serving.*

Illustrated opposite page 49

𝐵ROWNIES

MAKES 12

*Brownies keep nicely moist in an airtight tin for 4–5 days, and are
ideal for freezing.*

- 150 G/5 OZ BLOCK MARGARINE,
  AT ROOM TEMPERATURE
- 2 TBSP COCOA POWDER
- 150 G/5 OZ DARK MUSCOVADO
  SUGAR

- 2 EGGS, SIZE 3, BEATEN
- 50 G/2 OZ SELF-RAISING FLOUR
- 50 G/2 OZ SHELLED WALNUTS,
  ROUGHLY CHOPPED

1 Grease and line an 18cm/7inch square cake tin. Set the oven to 180°C/350°F/Gas 4.

2 Melt 50g/2oz of the margarine and stir in the cocoa, then set aside to cool slightly.

3 Cream the remaining margarine with the sugar until light and fluffy, then gradually beat in the eggs. Fold in the flour, walnuts and the cocoa mixture.

4 Spread the mixture in the tin and smooth the surface level. Bake for 35–45 minutes until firm to the touch in the centre. Leave to cool in the tin, then turn out, remove the lining paper and cut into twelve squares.

TO FREEZE: *Wrap in foil. Keeps for 3 months.*

Illustrated opposite page 48

$\mathcal{B}$LACK FOREST
KIRSCHTORTE

*Morello cherries, Kirsch, chocolate and cream provide a
combination that makes this one of the most popular cakes ever. It is
so irresistible I often serve it as a dinner party pudding, and it can
be prepared well ahead of time.*

- 5 EGGS, SIZE 2
- 175 G/6 OZ CASTER SUGAR
- 50 G/2 OZ PLAIN FLOUR
- 50 G/2 OZ COCOA POWDER
- 75 G/3 OZ BUTTER,
  MELTED AND COOLED
- **FILLING:**
- 1 × 425 G/15 OZ TIN
  MORELLO CHERRIES

- 5–6 TBSP KIRSCH
- 1 TBSP ARROWROOT
- 600 ML/1 PINT WHIPPING
  OR DOUBLE CREAM
- **DECORATION:**
- 225 G/8 OZ PLAIN CHOCOLATE
- 15–20 FRESH BLACK CHERRIES,
  IF AVAILABLE

1 Grease, base-line and flour two 20cm/8inch round sandwich tins. Set the oven to
180°C/350°F/Gas 4.

2 Put the eggs and sugar in a large heatproof bowl and set over a pan of hot water.
Whisk until the mixture is very thick and pale and firm enough to leave a ribbon trail
when the whisk is lifted. (You will need to whisk for about 8 minutes.) Remove from
the hot water and continue whisking until the mixture is almost tripled in bulk, about
10 minutes.

3 Sift the flour and cocoa together into the whisked mixture, and fold in very
gently. When the flour is almost incorporated, slowly pour in the melted butter in a
thin stream, folding gently. Try not to be heavy-handed at this stage or the finished
cake will be flat and heavy.

4 Divide the mixture between the tins and spread evenly. Bake for 25–30 minutes
or until springy to the touch in the centre, and slightly shrunken away from the sides
of the tins. Leave to cool in the tins, then turn out on to a wire rack and peel away the
lining paper. When cold, cut each cake in half horizontally using a thin sharp knife.

5 To make the filling, drain the syrup from the cherries into a bowl and mix in the
Kirsch. Blend half the syrup mixture with the arrowroot in a saucepan and boil until
thickened, stirring constantly. Cool, then stir in the drained cherries. Sprinkle the
remaining syrup over the four sponge layers.

6 Whip the cream until it forms soft peaks, then set half aside. Sandwich two layers
together with one-third of the remaining cream and place on a serving plate. Spread
another one-third on top, then spread over the cherries. Sandwich the remaining two
layers with the remaining third of cream and place on top, so that the cherries are
sandwiched in the centre layer.

Continued overleaf

7 Half fill a piping bag fitted with a star nozzle with some of the reserved cream, and spread the rest over the top and sides of the cake. Pipe the cream in two rings on top of the cake, then refrigerate.

8 Make chocolate curls (see page 184) with the plain chocolate, and press on to the sides of the cake. Place the fresh cherries between the two rings of piped cream. (If fresh cherries are not in season, decorate the top with extra chocolate curls.)

TO FREEZE: *Place in a rigid container, without the fresh cherries. Keeps for 3 months.*

Illustrated opposite page 48

$\mathcal{D}$ EVIL'S FOOD CAKE

This American cake is ideal for birthdays, covered in chocolate fudge icing (see page 168) or white seven-minute frosting (see page 166). Store it in an airtight tin for up to a week.

- 175 G/6 OZ PLAIN FLOUR
- 1 TSP BAKING POWDER
- ½ TSP BICARBONATE OF SODA
- 50 G/2 OZ COCOA POWDER
- 100 G/4 OZ BUTTER, AT ROOM TEMPERATURE

- 225 G/8 OZ DARK MUSCOVADO SUGAR
- 2 EGGS, SIZE 3
- 4 TBSP SOURED CREAM OR PLAIN YOGURT
- FILLING AND TOPPING (SEE STEP 5)

1 Grease and base-line two 20cm/8inch round sandwich tins. Set the oven to 190°C/375°F/Gas 5.

2 Sift the flour, baking powder and soda into a bowl. Mix the cocoa with 6 tbsp (90 ml) boiling water to make a smooth paste.

3 Cream the butter and sugar together until light and fluffy. Beat in the eggs, the soured cream or yogurt and the cocoa mixture, then fold in the sifted flour.

4 Divide the mixture evenly between the tins and level the tops. Bake for 30–35 minutes in the centre of the oven, until firm to the touch, cool in the tins for 3 minutes, then turn out on to wire racks to cool. Remove the lining paper from the cakes while still hot.

5 Sandwich the cakes together with chocolate fudge icing or seven-minute frosting, and spread over the top and sides as well.

TO FREEZE: *Wrap unfilled cake in foil. Keeps for 3 months.*

Illustrated opposite page 160

DECADENT CHOCOLATE ROULADE

This roulade makes a wonderful treat for tea or a dinner party pudding. It is always moist and delicious, and can easily be made the day before. Roulades have a tendency to crack, but I feel this improves their appearance – in life, nothing is perfect!

- 1 TBSP INSTANT COFFEE GRANULES
- 100 G/4 OZ PLAIN CHOCOLATE
- 4 EGGS, SIZE 2, SEPARATED
- 100 G/4 OZ CASTER SUGAR
- CASTER OR ICING SUGAR, TO DREDGE

- **FILLING:**
- 300 ML/½ PINT DOUBLE CREAM
- 1 TBSP GRAND MARNIER OR OTHER ORANGE LIQUEUR

1 Grease and line a 28 × 33cm/11 × 13inch Swiss roll tin with non-stick silicone paper (see lining a Swiss roll tin, page 32). Set the oven to 180°C/350°F/Gas 4.

2 Make the coffee into a smooth paste with 1 tbsp water. Melt the chocolate gently in a heatproof bowl set over warm water or in the microwave oven, then leave to cool slightly.

3 Whisk the egg yolks and sugar together in a bowl over hot water, using an electric beater, until thick and pale. Remove from heat, then stir in the cooled coffee and chocolate. Whisk the egg whites until stiff. Fold 2 tbsp into the chocolate mixture to loosen it, then fold in the remaining whites carefully, trying to keep the mixture as light as possible.

4 Spread the mixture in the tin and bake in the centre of the oven for about 15 minutes. The top of the cake will be crusty, but underneath it will be very moist. Place the tin on a wire rack, cover with a clean, damp tea towel, and leave overnight. This will make the crust soften.

5 Sprinkle a large sheet of greaseproof paper with caster or sifted icing sugar. Remove the tea towel, then turn out the cake on to the sugared paper. Peel off the lining paper and trim the crusty edges of the cake.

6 Whip the cream until stiff, then fold in the orange liqueur. Spread over the cake, then roll up carefully, using the paper to help you lift and roll. Place on a serving dish and dust with more sugar. You may find the roulade cracks on the surface, but this is quite normal. Decorate with chocolate curls or leaves (see page 184) if you want to cover any bad cracks.

Not suitable for freezing.

Illustrated opposite page 160

*D*ELICIOUSLY MOIST
BIRTHDAY CAKE

This dark, moist chocolate cake is really easy to make and keeps well. I often use it as a base for birthday cakes as it can be made a few days ahead, which gives plenty of time to concentrate on the decoration.

- 75 G/3 OZ COCOA POWDER
- 175 G/6 OZ BUTTER, AT ROOM TEMPERATURE
- 275 G/10 OZ CASTER SUGAR
- 3 EGGS, SIZE 3, BEATEN
- 275 G/10 OZ PLAIN FLOUR
- 1 ½ TSP BICARBONATE OF SODA
- ½ TSP BAKING POWDER
- FILLING AND TOPPING (SEE STEP 6)

1 Dissolve the cocoa in 350 ml/12 fl oz boiling water, then leave until cold – this will take about 25 minutes.

2 Grease and line a 20cm/8inch round deep cake tin. Set the oven to 180°C/350°F/ Gas 4.

3 Cream the butter and sugar together until light and fluffy, then gradually beat in the eggs, adding a teaspoon of flour with each addition, to keep the mixture smooth.

4 Sift the remaining flour, the bicarbonate of soda and baking powder together into the creamed mixture. Fold in with the cocoa mixture until smooth.

5 Pour the mixture into the tin. Bake for about 1 hour or until firm to the touch. Leave to cool in the tin for 5 minutes, then turn out on to a wire rack to cool completely.

6 Sandwich the cake together with raspberry or apricot jam, or cream flavoured with liqueur. Cover with cream and chocolate curls (see page 184) or fondant icing (see page 164).

TO FREEZE: *Wrap undecorated cake in foil or freezer bag. Keeps for up to 2 months.*

SQUIDGY CHOCOLATE FUDGE LAYER

This really is one of the richest of cakes – chocolate cake with a rich chocolate ganache filling. Sheer heaven! I'm informed that chocolate eaten in the morning is not quite as fattening as that eaten later in the day, so a slice for morning coffee is perfectly O.K.

- 250 G/9 OZ PLAIN CHOCOLATE
- 1 TBSP INSTANT COFFEE POWDER
- 2 TBSP BRANDY
- 4 EGGS, SIZE 3
- 1 TSP VANILLA ESSENCE
- 50 G/2 OZ SOFT LIGHT BROWN SUGAR

- 1 TBSP CORNFLOUR
- 25 G/1 OZ COCOA POWDER
- COCOA POWDER, TO DREDGE
- **CHOCOLATE GANACHE:**
- 150 ML/¼ PINT DOUBLE CREAM
- 100 G/4 OZ PLAIN OR MILK CHOCOLATE

1 Lightly oil a 900g/2lb loaf tin and line the base and sides with non-stick silicone paper. Set the oven to 180°C/350°F/Gas 4.

2 Break the chocolate into pieces and put in a heatproof bowl. Add the coffee powder, brandy and 2 tbsp water. Place over a pan of warm water, or in the microwave oven, and heat gently until melted. Stir together, then leave to cool.

3 Whisk the eggs, vanilla essence, sugar and cornflour together until very thick. Fold in the cooled chocolate mixture. Sift in the cocoa powder and fold in.

4 Pour the mixture into the prepared tin and bake for 1 hour to 1 hour 10 minutes or until a skewer inserted into the middle comes out clean. Leave to cool in the tin for 10 minutes, then turn out on to a wire rack to cool completely. The cake keeps well, and becomes softer after 1 day, so keep it overnight, if possible, before cutting it into layers.

5 To make the ganache filling, place the cream in a small saucepan and bring to the boil. Remove from the heat and add the chocolate, broken into pieces. Stir until completely melted, then return to the heat and bring back to the boil. Pour into a bowl and cool. If made ahead of time, keep in the refrigerator until needed, then soften at room temperature for about 1 hour before use.

6 To assemble the cake, cut carefully into three layers lengthways and sandwich back together with the ganache filling, spread or piped. Sift over cocoa powder and decorate with chocolate leaves (see page 184), if liked.

TO FREEZE: *Freeze unfilled cake in a rigid container, as it is delicate. Keeps for 3 months.*

ℛICH CHOCOLATE AND ALMOND LAYER CAKE

A wickedly luxurious chocolate cake sandwiched together with almond cream and coated in a glossy layer of chocolate.

- 100 G/4 OZ PLAIN CHOCOLATE
- 4 EGGS, SIZE 3, SEPARATED
- FEW DROPS ALMOND ESSENCE
- 175 G/6 OZ BUTTER, AT ROOM TEMPERATURE
- 175 G/6 OZ DARK MUSCOVADO SUGAR
- 175 G/6 OZ SELF-RAISING FLOUR
- 25 G/1 OZ GROUND ALMONDS
- 25 G/1 OZ COCOA POWDER
- 3–4 TBSP MILK

FILLING:
- 150 ML/¼ PINT DOUBLE OR WHIPPING CREAM
- 3–4 TBSP AMARETTO OR OTHER ALMOND LIQUEUR

TOPPING:
- 175 G/6 OZ PLAIN CHOCOLATE
- 150 ML/¼ PINT DOUBLE CREAM
- 50 G/2 OZ PLAIN CHOCOLATE, MADE INTO CURLS (SEE PAGE 184)
- 8 WHOLE, SKINNED ALMONDS
- 1 TBSP COCOA POWDER

1 Set the oven to 180°C/350°F/Gas 4. Grease and base-line a 20cm/8inch round loose-based or spring-clip cake tin.

2 Break up the chocolate into pieces and put into a heatproof bowl with 4 tbsp boiling water. Melt over a pan of warm water until smooth. Remove from the heat and beat in the egg yolks and almond essence.

3 Cream the butter and sugar together until light and fluffy, then beat in the chocolate mixture. Sift the flour, almonds and cocoa together, then fold into the creamed mixture with the milk. Whisk the egg whites until they form soft peaks. Fold 2 tbsp into the mixture to loosen it, then fold in the remaining egg whites gently.

4 Spoon the mixture into the prepared tin. Bake in the centre of the oven for 50–60 minutes or until firm to the touch in the centre. Leave to cool in the tin, then turn out and peel away the lining paper. Slice the cake into three layers horizontally using a long sharp knife.

5 To make the filling, whip the cream with the liqueur until stiff. Use to sandwich the cake layers together.

6 To make the topping, break the chocolate into pieces and melt gently in a heatproof bowl over a pan of warm water. Stir in the cream, then quickly spread over the top and sides of the cake, to give a smooth finish. Press the chocolate curls round the side of the cake whilst still wet.

7 Dip the almonds in any leftover chocolate mixture to coat them. Leave to dry, then roll the nuts in the cocoa powder. Press the almonds into the top of the cake to decorate.

TO FREEZE: *Wrap filled cake in foil. Keeps for 3 months. Decorate after thawing.*

Illustrated opposite page 160

*Spoon alternative cake colours
around ring mould*

*When cooked, loosen edges
and turn out*

AUSTRIAN CHOCOLATE AND ORANGE RING CAKE

*This moist ring cake combines the flavours of chocolate and orange
which complement each other deliciously. For extra luxury, sprinkle
the cake with an orange liqueur before covering.*

- 50 G/2 OZ PLAIN CHOCOLATE
- 225 G/8 OZ UNSALTED BUTTER, AT ROOM TEMPERATURE
- 225 G/8 OZ SOFT BROWN SUGAR
- 4 EGGS, SIZE 2
- 225 G/8 OZ PLAIN FLOUR
- 2 TSP BAKING POWDER
- PINCH SALT
- 50 G/2 OZ GROUND ALMONDS

- FINELY GRATED ZEST ½ ORANGE
- 2 TBSP FRESH ORANGE JUICE
- **CHOCOLATE ICING AND DECORATION:**
- 175 G/6 OZ PLAIN CHOCOLATE
- 100 G/4 OZ UNSALTED BUTTER
- 50 G/2 OZ MILK CHOCOLATE

1 Set the oven to 180°C/350°F/Gas 4. Lightly butter a 1.7 litre/3 pint ring mould.

2 Break up the chocolate and melt in a small heatproof bowl set over a pan of warm water, or in the microwave oven. Add 1 tbsp water and stir, then remove from the heat to cool.

3 Cream the butter and sugar together until light and fluffy. Beat in the eggs one at a time, adding a little flour with each to prevent curdling.

4 Sift the remaining flour, the baking powder, salt and almonds together, then sift again into the creamed mixture. Stir in the orange zest and juice.

5 Place half the mixture in a separate bowl and stir in the cooled melted chocolate. Place large spoonfuls of each mixture alternately in the ring mould. Smooth the top level, then draw a knife through the mixture, turning the mould clockwise at the same time to swirl the two mixtures together. Level the top again.

6 Bake for 50 minutes to 1 hour or until a warmed skewer inserted into the deepest part comes out clean. Leave in the tin to cool for 3 minutes then turn out on a wire rack to cool.

7 To make the chocolate icing, break the plain chocolate into a heatproof bowl and add 2 tbsp water and the butter. Set over a pan of warm water, or in the microwave oven, and melt, stirring occasionally. Pour the icing over the cold cake and quickly spread it evenly over the sides. Leave to set for 1 hour.

8 To decorate, melt the milk chocolate, place in a small paper piping bag (see page 182) and snip a small hole in the end. Drizzle the chocolate over the cake in a zig-zag pattern and leave to set.

TO FREEZE: *Wrap undecorated cake in foil. Keeps for 2 months. Ice after thawing.*

RIGHT (from top to bottom): Black Forest Kirschtorte (see page 41); Austrian Chocolate and Orange Ring Cake (see above); Brownies (see page 40).

Illustrated opposite page 48

CHOCOLATE MINCEMEAT CAKE

Make this cake around Christmas time. It's based on a jar of mincemeat, but you can vary the fruit and nuts, and so on, according to whatever is in the store-cupboard. It makes a good last-minute Christmas or New Year party cake, and will keep well for up to 2 weeks.

- 100 G/4 OZ BUTTER, AT ROOM TEMPERATURE
- 100 G/4 OZ DARK MUSCOVADO SUGAR
- 3 EGGS, SIZE 3, BEATEN
- 225 G/8 OZ WHOLEMEAL SELF-RAISING FLOUR
- 1 TSP MIXED SPICE
- 1 × 400 G/14 OZ JAR MINCEMEAT
- 75 G/3 OZ RAISINS
- 50 G/2 OZ GLACÉ CHERRIES, RINSED, DRIED AND HALVED
- 100 G/4 OZ PLAIN CHOCOLATE, COARSELY GRATED
- 50 G/2 OZ SHELLED PECAN NUTS OR WALNUTS, ROUGHLY CHOPPED (OPTIONAL)
- TOPPING (OPTIONAL, SEE STEP 5)

1 Set the oven to 160°C/325°F/Gas 3. Grease and line a 20cm/8inch round deep cake tin or an 18cm/7inch square tin.

2 Cream the butter and sugar together until light and fluffy, then beat in the eggs gradually, adding a little flour with each addition.

3 Sift the remaining flour and spice into the bowl, add the bran from the sieve and fold in with all the remaining ingredients. Spoon into the prepared tin, make a slight hollow in the centre to allow for even rising, and spread the sides level.

4 Bake in the centre of the oven for just under 2 hours. Test with a skewer: if it comes out clean, the cake is done. Leave to cool in the tin.

5 If liked, cover with a thin layer of almond paste (see page 160) and royal or fondant icing (see page 162 or 164); alternatively brush the surface with honey and sprinkle with demerara sugar.

TO FREEZE: *Wrap undecorated cake tightly in foil. Keeps for 3 months.*

Illustrated opposite page 96

LEFT (from top to bottom): Spicy Date and Rum Cake (see page 63); Sachertorte (see page 39); Honey Cake (see page 60).

Chocolate Yule Log
(BÛCHE DE NOËL)

SERVES 10

In France, the Bûche de Noël, *or Christmas log, is traditionally eaten as the main festive cake. In Britain, we tend to serve it for family teas and gatherings together with a classic rich fruit Christmas cake – oh, we are greedy!*

- 90 G/3½ OZ SELF-RAISING FLOUR
- 2 TBSP COCOA POWDER
- PINCH SALT
- 4 EGGS, SIZE 3

- 100 G/4 OZ CASTER SUGAR
- FILLING AND TOPPING (SEE STEP 6)
- ICING SUGAR, TO DREDGE

1 Set the oven to 220°C/425°F/Gas 7. Oil and line a 23 × 33cm/9 × 13inch Swiss roll tin with oiled greaseproof paper.

2 Sift together the flour, cocoa and salt.

3 Place the eggs and sugar in a large heatproof bowl and set over a pan of hot water. Whisk until thick, remove from the hot water and continue whisking until the mixture is very thick and pale and firm enough to leave a ribbon trail when the whisk is lifted. Fold in half the flour mixture. Fold in the remaining flour with 1 tbsp hot water.

4 Pour the mixture into the prepared tin and spread evenly. Bake for about 10 minutes or until firm to the touch.

5 Have ready a dampened tea towel spread out flat and a large sheet of greaseproof paper on top of it, dusted with caster sugar. Turn out the sponge on to the paper, peel away the lining paper and trim the crusty edges quickly with a sharp knife. Loosely roll up the sponge, rolling the sugared paper inside. Leave the cake to cool, keeping it in a nice rounded shape.

6 To decorate, cover and fill with chocolate buttercream (see page 170) or crème au beurre (see page 167). Mark on lines with a fork to resemble wood, sprinkle with icing sugar, and decorate with holly or Christmas novelties.

TO FREEZE: *Wrap in foil or in a rigid container. Keeps for 3 months. Fill and ice after thawing.*

Illustrated opposite page 16

CARIBBEAN CAROB CAKE

I've included this delicious carob cake for those poor unfortunates who cannot eat chocolate – a fate worse than death as far as I'm concerned! The combination of pineapple and carob makes the cake taste very chocolatey, and you'll fool your guests into thinking it's the real thing.

- 2 TBSP CAROB POWDER
- 225 G/8 OZ SOFT VEGETABLE MARGARINE, AT ROOM TEMPERATURE
- 225 G/8 OZ SOFT LIGHT BROWN SUGAR
- 4 EGGS, SIZE 3
- 1 TSP VANILLA ESSENCE
- 225 G/8 OZ SELF-RAISING FLOUR

- 50 G/2 OZ CAROB BAR, TO DECORATE
- **FILLING:**
- 100 G/4 OZ FULL-FAT SOFT CHEESE
- 450 G/1 LB FROMAGE FRAIS
- 1 TBSP CASTER SUGAR
- 1 × 425 G/15 OZ TIN CRUSHED PINEAPPLE, WELL DRAINED

1 Grease and base-line a 22cm/8½–9inch round deep cake tin. Set the oven to 180°C/350°F/Gas 4.

2 Mix the carob powder with 4 tbsp cold water. Cream the margarine and sugar together until light and fluffy, then gradually whisk in the carob mixture, the eggs and vanilla essence. Gently fold in the flour.

3 Spread the mixture in the tin, and make a slight hollow in the centre. Bake for about 1 hour or until a skewer inserted in the middle comes out clean, with no mixture sticking to it.

4 Leave in the tin until almost cold, then turn out and peel away the lining paper. Cut the cake horizontally into three layers.

5 To make the filling, soften the cheese in a bowl, then beat in the fromage frais and sugar. Mix in the crushed pineapple.

6 Use one-third of the filling to sandwich the cake layers together. Spread the remaining filling over the top and sides of the cake. Coarsely grate the carob bar and sprinkle over the top and sides of the cake. Refrigerate until needed.

TO FREEZE: *Wrap undecorated cake in foil. Keeps for up to 2 months.*

SPICY CAKES

*F*rom the time of the ancient Greeks and Romans, spices have been highly prized, and used in baking. The opening of trade routes in the Middle Ages brought spices like ginger, cloves, and cinnamon to Europe, which featured in the recipes of the rich. Sweet spice cakes were eaten as a luxury, and many of the cakes we know today, particularly continental ones, have their origins in these times. Spices were also thought to be highly medicinal, and cakes like gingerbread were taken as part of a 'cure'.

Today, spices are cheap, plentiful and easily available. They can provide a wealth of smooth, warm and mellow flavours to cakes and breads. Baking would be very dull indeed without the existence of cinnamon, nutmeg and all the wonderful spices that add those extra flavours and aromas we all love. No longer do you have to be rich or royal to enjoy the privilege of spices, so make the most of the extensive ranges sold in the shops today.

SPICY CAKES

KEEPING SPICES

Most of the seeds, bark and roots that we buy as spices are dried. They have a fairly long shelf life, but will not keep well indefinitely so follow these tips for storing them:

☞ Spices gradually lose their aroma, and some are past their best in three months, so buy your spices in small quantities, only when you need them.

☞ A pretty spice rack looks very nice in a kitchen, but remember the spices in it are deteriorating quickly.

☞ Both light and heat affect the flavour, so if you do use clear glass jars keep them stored away in a drawer cupboard, out of the light.

☞ Small tins with tightly fitting lids are ideal containers preferable to glass if you can find them.

☞ If your kitchen is hot and steamy or you have an Aga, or oven that is constantly burning, then find a cooler place for your spices.

☞ Don't tip spices straight from the jar into hot or steamy mixtures. The steam will go into the jar, causing the spices to get damp and quickly deteriorate.

☞ Whole spices can be freshly ground in a small electric mill or pestle and mortar. They have a much stronger flavour and aroma than the ground ones, so use them more sparingly.

☞ Nutmeg can be ground freshly into cake mixtures by grating the whole spice on a very fine grater. The flavour will be far superior than that of the dried, ground variety, but do remember the extra strength it has and cut down the amount used in the recipe.

☞ If you do use freshly ground spices in recipes, cut down the amount stated in the recipe by half.

$\mathscr{P}$ASSION CAKE

Passion or carrot cakes have been national favourites in the USA for years, and Mrs Beeton was fond of using carrots in jams and puddings. Luckily, the carrot has made a comeback with the 'healthy eating' trend. I love carrot cake with its spicy, mellow flavour and moist texture. It is popular at children's parties, too.

- 275 G/10 OZ PLAIN FLOUR
- PINCH SALT
- 1 TSP BICARBONATE OF SODA
- 2 TSP BAKING POWDER
- 2 TSP GROUND CINNAMON
- 175 G/6 OZ SOFT BROWN SUGAR
- 50 G/2 OZ SHELLED WALNUTS, CHOPPED
- 3 EGGS, SIZE 3
- 2 RIPE BANANAS, MASHED
- 150 G/5 OZ CARROTS, FINELY GRATED
- 175 ML/6 FL OZ VEGETABLE, CORN OR SUNFLOWER OIL
- SOFT CHEESE ICING (SEE PAGE 167)
- DECORATION (SEE STEP 4)

1 Grease and base-line a 22cm/8½inch loose-based or spring-clip cake tin. Set the oven to 180°C/350°F/Gas 4.

2 Sift the flour, salt, bicarbonate of soda, baking powder and cinnamon into a bowl and add the sugar and nuts. Add the eggs and bananas and beat well, then mix in the carrots and oil.

3 Spoon the mixture into the tin. Bake for 50 minutes to 1 hour or until firm to the touch in the centre. Leave to cool in the tin.

4 Turn out the cake and cover the top with soft cheese icing. Sprinkle with chopped walnuts, or use whole ones and place in a circle on top; alternatively make tiny carrots from coloured almond paste (see page 160), and place in a circle on top.

TO FREEZE: *Freeze with or without cheese icing, wrapped in foil. Keeps for 3 months un-iced, 6 weeks iced.*

Illustrated opposite page 64

Cinnamon-crusted

CHEESECAKE

Not all cheesecakes have to be made with double cream and full-fat soft cheese. This recipe is my favourite, given to me by an Austrian chef, and is light and feathery. My guests usually ask for seconds!

- 75 G/3 OZ BUTTER
- 1 ½ TSP GROUND CINNAMON
- 225 G/8 OZ CAKE CRUMBS, FINELY GRATED
- ICING SUGAR, TO DREDGE
- FRESH FRUIT, TO DECORATE
- **FILLING:**
- 6 EGGS, SIZE 3, SEPARATED
- 225 G/8 OZ CASTER SUGAR

- FINELY GRATED ZEST AND JUICE 1 LEMON
- 450 G/1 LB LOW-FAT SOFT CHEESE OR CURD CHEESE
- 225 ML/8 FL OZ PLAIN SET YOGURT
- 2 TBSP PLAIN FLOUR
- 1 TBSP BRANDY, RUM OR SHERRY

1 Line the base and sides of a 23cm/9inch loose-based or spring-clip cake tin with a sheet of foil, shiny side towards you. Lightly grease the foil. Set the oven to 180°C/350°F/Gas 4.

2 Melt the butter in a pan over a low heat or in the microwave oven. Stir the cinnamon into the cake crumbs, then mix into the melted butter. Press the crumb mixture over the base and up the sides of the tin.

3 Whisk the egg yolks with the sugar until light and fluffy, then stir in the lemon zest and juice, cheese, yogurt, flour and alcohol. Whisk the egg whites until stiff and fold into the cheese mixture.

4 Pour the filling into the crumb crust. Bake for 1 hour, then turn off the heat. Leave the cake in the cooling oven for another hour, but check it doesn't get too brown. Cool the cheesecake in the tin, then refrigerate in the tin until needed.

5 To serve, remove the sides of the tin and carefully peel away the foil. Dust the top with sifted icing sugar and decorate with fresh fruit – redcurrants, raspberries or strawberries, and kiwi fruit look pretty.

Not suitable for freezing.

ORKNEY GINGERBREAD

This is a good-keeping cake for the cake tin, and it improves with a few days' storage. It is eaten in Scotland spread with butter and sometimes served with cheese or apples. Don't be put off by the very wet texture before baking; the mixture is supposed to be like this. This is a quickly made cake, and easy enough for children who want to lend a hand.

- 150 G/5 OZ PLAIN FLOUR
- PINCH SALT
- 1 TSP GROUND GINGER
- 1 TSP GROUND CINNAMON
- 2 TSP BAKING POWDER
- 150 G/5 OZ PORRIDGE OATS
- 175 G/6 OZ DARK MUSCOVADO SUGAR

- 6 TBSP DARK TREACLE
- 100 G/4 OZ BUTTER OR BLOCK MARGARINE
- 1 EGG, SIZE 3, BEATEN
- 300 ML/½ PINT MILK
- 100 G/4 OZ RAISINS
- 50 G/2 OZ SLIVERED ALMONDS

1 Set the oven to 180°C/350°F/Gas 4. Grease and then line a 20cm/8inch round deep cake tin.

2 Sift the flour, salt, spices and baking powder into a large bowl and stir in the oats and sugar.

3 Gently heat the treacle and fat together in a saucepan or the microwave oven until the fat has melted. Stir into the flour mixture with the egg and milk. Add the raisins and nuts and mix well. The mixture will have a very wet consistency.

4 Pour into the cake tin. Bake in the centre of the oven for 1¼–1½ hours or until firm to the touch in the centre. Leave to cool in the tin, then turn out and peel off the lining paper. Store in an airtight tin until required.

TO FREEZE: *Wrap in foil. Keeps for 2 months.*

ℋONEY CAKE

*The ancient Greeks and Romans believed that honey would give
them a longer and healthier life, and they liked to eat baked small
cakes made with honey instead of sugar. This modern version will
be just as popular today.*

* 300 ML/½ PINT CLEAR HONEY
* 75 G/3 OZ BUTTER
* 350 G/12 OZ WHOLEMEAL FLOUR
* 2 TSP MIXED SPICE
* 1 TSP BICARBONATE OF SODA
* 50 G/2 OZ CHOPPED CANDIED
  MIXED PEEL

* 3 EGGS, SIZE 3
* 3 TBSP MILK
* FINELY GRATED ZEST
  1 LEMON
* 50 G/2 OZ FLAKED ALMONDS

1 Set the oven to 170°C/325°F/Gas 3. Grease and line a 20cm/8inch square cake tin
or 18cm/7inch round deep cake tin.

2 Spoon out 4 tbsp honey and reserve. Pour the rest of the honey into a saucepan,
add the butter and heat until melted, keeping the heat low.

3 Sift the flour, spice and soda into a bowl and add any remaining bran left in the
sieve. Stir in the mixed peel. Beat the eggs, milk and zest together, then add to the
dry mixture with the cooled honey. Beat together until well combined, then pour into
the cake tin.

4 Sprinkle over the almonds. Bake for about 1¼ hours or until firm and a skewer
inserted in the middle comes out clean.

5 Leave to cool in the tin for 5 minutes, then turn out on to a wire rack. Prick the
top of the cake with a skewer and brush over the reserved honey while the cake is
still warm.

TO FREEZE: *Wrap tightly in foil. Keeps for 2 months.*

Illustrated opposite page 49

$\mathcal{A}$PFELKUCHEN

This rich, moist cake has a shortbread-like quality. Serve it hot as a pudding, or cold as a cake.

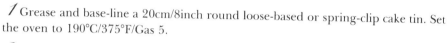

- 300 G/11 OZ SELF-RAISING FLOUR
- 200 G/7 OZ CASTER SUGAR
- 225 G/8 OZ BUTTER, AT ROOM TEMPERATURE
- 1 EGG, SIZE 2
- 450 G/1LB COOKING APPLES, PEELED, CORED AND SLICED

- 50 G/2 OZ SULTANAS
- 1 TBSP CLEAR HONEY
- 1½ TSP GROUND CINNAMON
- 100 G/4 OZ FLAKED ALMONDS
- ICING SUGAR, TO DREDGE

1 Grease and base-line a 20cm/8inch round loose-based or spring-clip cake tin. Set the oven to 190°C/375°F/Gas 5.

2 Place the flour and sugar in a bowl and rub in the butter until the mixture resembles fine breadcrumbs. Stir in the egg and knead lightly to make a smooth dough. Divide in half and press half into the tin to line the base, levelling as much as possible. Bake for 15–20 minutes until golden.

3 Meanwhile, place the apples, sultanas, honey, cinnamon and 2 tbsp water in a saucepan. Cover and cook for 5–6 minutes. Cool, then spoon on to the cooked pastry base.

4 Roll out the remaining dough to 1cm/½inch thick. Cut out a round the size of the tin. Scatter 25g/1oz almonds on top of the apple mixture, then press the dough round on top. Sprinkle over the remaining almonds.

5 Bake for a further 30 minutes or until the pastry top is firm. Leave to cool in the tin, then turn out and sprinkle with sifted icing sugar to serve.

TO FREEZE: *Wrap in foil. Keeps for 6 months.*

RICH GINGER CAKE

A truly delicious, sticky cake that improves with keeping. Wrap it in greaseproof paper, then keep in a tin for 2–3 days. Beware of prying hands!

- 100 G/4 OZ BUTTER OR BLOCK MARGARINE, AT ROOM TEMPERATURE
- 100 G/4 OZ SOFT BROWN SUGAR
- 2 EGGS, SIZE 3
- 1 TBSP GOLDEN SYRUP
- 1 TBSP DARK TREACLE
- 225 G/8 OZ PLAIN FLOUR
- ½ TSP GROUND GINGER
- ½ TSP BAKING POWDER
- 100 G/4 OZ PRESERVED STEM GINGER, CHOPPED
- **DECORATION** (OPTIONAL):
- 150 ML/¼ PINT DOUBLE CREAM, WHIPPED
- 10–12 BRANDY SNAPS

1 Set the oven to 190°C/375°F/Gas 5. Grease and line an 18cm/7inch round deep cake tin.

2 Cream the fat and sugar together until light and fluffy. Beat in the eggs one at a time, followed by the syrup and treacle.

3 Sift in the flour, ground ginger and baking powder, then fold in gently with the preserved ginger. Spoon into the tin and smooth level.

4 Bake for about 1 hour or until firm in the centre. Leave to cool in the tin for 5 minutes, then turn out on to a wire rack to cool completely.

5 To decorate, pipe cream into the brandy snaps and spread the remaining cream over the top of the cake. Arrange the brandy snaps on the cream in a circle like the spokes of a wheel.

TO FREEZE: *Wrap undecorated cake in foil. Keeps for 3 months.*

$\mathcal{S}$PICY DATE AND RUM CAKE

The flavours of dark rum, dates and spices blend together to make this a favourite for the cake tin. It will keep for 3 weeks.

- 225 G/8 OZ BUTTER, AT ROOM TEMPERATURE
- 175 G/6 OZ SOFT LIGHT BROWN SUGAR
- 3 TBSP DARK TREACLE
- 4 EGGS, SIZE 3, BEATEN
- 350 G/12 OZ WHOLEMEAL SELF-RAISING FLOUR
- 2 TSP GROUND NUTMEG
- 2 TSP GROUND CINNAMON
- 2 TSP GROUND GINGER
- 50 G/2 OZ FLAKED ALMONDS
- 225 G/8 OZ STONED DATES, ROUGHLY CHOPPED
- 350 G/12 OZ MIXED DRIED FRUIT
- 3 TBSP DARK RUM
- TOPPING (SEE STEP 4)

1 Set the oven to 150°C/300°F/Gas 2. Grease and line a 20cm/8inch square cake tin or a 23cm/9inch round deep cake tin, using a double layer of greaseproof paper.

2 Cream the butter and sugar together until light and fluffy, then beat in the treacle. Beat in the eggs gradually, adding a spoonful of flour with each one. Sift the remaining flour and the spices into the mixture, adding any bran left in the sieve, and fold in with the almonds, dates, fruit and rum.

3 Spoon into the tin and smooth level. Bake for about 2 hours or until firm to the touch in the centre. Leave to cool in the tin for 10 minutes, then turn out on to a wire rack to cool completely.

4 Sprinkle over more dark rum for extra flavour if liked. Spread with apricot glaze (see page 169) and sprinkle with demerara sugar, or cover with almond paste (see page 160) and ice with fondant or royal icing (see page 164 or 162).

TO FREEZE: *Wrap undecorated in foil. Keeps for 4 months.*

Illustrated opposite page 49

SCANDINAVIAN SPICED APPLE CAKE

The flavours of apples and warm spices have always complemented each other. They blend well together in this unusual, moist cake.

- 100 G/4 OZ BUTTER, AT ROOM TEMPERATURE
- 225 G/8 OZ DARK MUSCOVADO SUGAR
- 2 EGGS, SIZE 3, BEATEN
- 225 G/8 OZ WHOLEMEAL SELF-RAISING FLOUR
- 1/4 TSP SALT
- 1 TSP GROUND CINNAMON
- 1/4 TSP GROUND CLOVES
- 1 TSP VANILLA ESSENCE
- 275 G/10 OZ COOKING APPLES, PEELED, CORED AND COARSELY GRATED

TOPPING:
- 1 TBSP CLEAR HONEY
- 1–2 TBSP TOASTED FLAKED ALMONDS

1 Set the oven to 180°C/350°F/Gas 4. Grease and line a 20cm/8inch round deep cake tin or a 18cm/7inch square cake tin.

2 Cream the butter and sugar together until light and fluffy, then beat in the eggs one at a time. Sift the flour, salt and spices into the creamed mixture, add the bran from the sieve and fold in with the vanilla essence and apples.

3 Spread the mixture in the prepared tin and level the top. Bake for about 1¼ hours or until lightly browned and the sides of the cake are beginning to shrink away from the tin.

4 Leave to cool in the tin for 5 minutes, then turn out on to a wire rack to cool completely.

5 Brush the top of the cake with the honey, then arrange the nuts over. Eat within 2–3 days, sliced and buttered.

Not suitable for freezing.

RIGHT (from top to bottom): Apricot, Caraway and Brandy Ring (see page 68); Passion Cake (see page 57); Scandinavian Spiced Apple Cake (see above).

$\mathcal{G}$INGERBREAD HOUSE

'Crack, crack, crunch,
who is nibbling at my house?'
(Hansel and Gretel, Grimm's Fairy Tales).

*The witch won't get you if you eat this gingerbread house,
but it does deserve to be on display for a few days at Christmas first,
as a charming centrepiece.*

- 3 TBSP GOLDEN SYRUP OR HONEY
- 175 G/6 OZ BUTTER, AT ROOM TEMPERATURE
- 175 G/6 OZ MUSCOVADO SUGAR
- 3 EGG YOLKS, SIZE 3
- 700 G/1 ½ LB PLAIN FLOUR
- 1 ½ TSP BICARBONATE OF SODA
- 2 TSP GROUND GINGER
- 1 TSP MIXED SPICE
- 1 TBSP COCOA POWDER
- 9–10 TBSP MILK
- **DECORATION:**
- 900 G/2 LB ROYAL ICING (SEE PAGE 162)

1 Oil 4 baking sheets. Set the oven to 180°C/350°F/Gas 4. Copy the templates, seen below, out on to card and cut out.

2 Melt the golden syrup or honey in a small pan or in the microwave oven. Cream the butter and sugar together until light and fluffy, then beat in the egg yolks one at a time. Sift in the flour, soda, spices and cocoa and fold in with a spoon. Add the syrup or honey and enough milk to make a soft but not sticky dough. Knead until smooth.

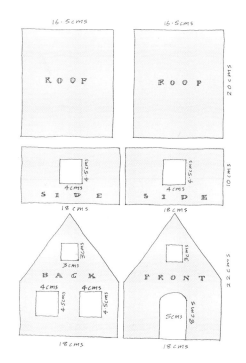

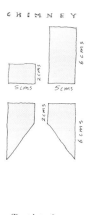

Templates for gingerbread house

Continued overleaf

LEFT: Gingerbread House (see above).

*Cut out dough pieces
using templates*

Assemble sides of house first

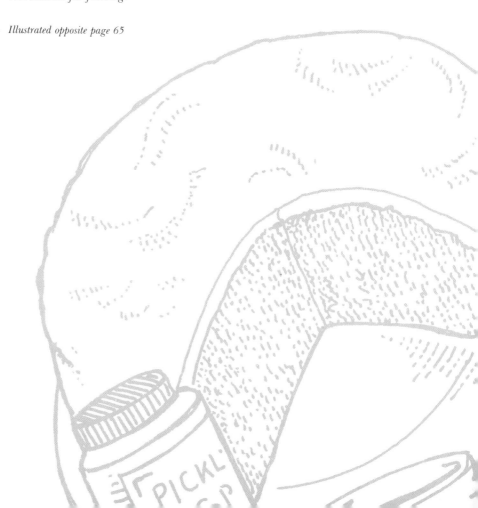

3 Roll out the dough between two sheets of non-stick paper on a floured surface to about 5mm /¼inch thick. Cut out the pieces using the templates: (1 front of house with windows, 1 back of house, 2 roof panels, 2 sides of house with windows, 1 door, 12 window shutters, 1 door and 4 chimney pieces). Lift them carefully on to the baking sheets (use a fish slice to help).

4 Bake for 15 minutes. Allow to cool on the sheets for the windows to set. Check the shapes against the templates and if necessary trim them to shape whilst still warm. Leave on a wire rack until firm enough to handle – 4–5 hours.

5 To assemble the house, fill a greaseproof paper piping bag (see page 182) with royal icing. Snip the end and pipe along the base and side edges of the frame. Fix in position on a 30cm/12inch square cake board. Support with a cardboard food pack or tin until dry. When the walls are set and firm, fix on the two roof panels, and hold in place until firm. Stick the chimney together and position in place with icing. Attach the lintel over the door, and set the door in position, slightly ajar. Stick the shutters to the lower windows. Leave the house to dry out until firm before decorating.

6 Pipe on roof tiles with royal icing, dripping it over the sides for a snow effect. Pipe on royal icing round the windows.

Not suitable for freezing.

Illustrated opposite page 65

*Decorate house with piped
royal icing*

NUREMBERG NUT CAKE

This lovely cake is a collection of all of my favourite things – nuts, chocolate, spices and honey. It is so rich I often cut it into small squares and serve it as a petits fours cake with coffee.

* 100 G/4 OZ SHELLED HAZELNUTS OR PECAN NUTS
* 100 G/4 OZ WHOLE SKINNED ALMONDS
* 100 G/4 OZ CHOPPED CANDIED MIXED PEEL
* 100 G/4 OZ GLACÉ CHERRIES, HALVED
* 100 G/4 OZ SULTANAS OR RAISINS

* 50 G/2 OZ PLAIN FLOUR
* 40 G/1 ½ OZ COCOA POWDER
* 1 TSP GROUND CINNAMON
* ¼ TSP GROUND CLOVES
* ¼ TSP GROUND GINGER
* PINCH GROUND CARDAMOM (OPTIONAL)
* 75 G/3 OZ MUSCOVADO SUGAR
* 100 G/4 OZ CLEAR HONEY
* ICING SUGAR, TO DREDGE

1 Set the oven to 180°C/350°F/Gas 4. Line a 20cm/8inch round deep cake tin or an 18cm/7inch square tin with non-stick silicone paper, or rice paper if you have it.

2 Mix the whole nuts, peel, cherries and sultanas in a bowl. Sift in the flour, cocoa and spices and stir well.

3 Warm the sugar and honey together in a saucepan until the grains of sugar have dissolved. Stir into the fruit and nut mixture.

4 Pour into the lined tin and spread level. Bake for 30 minutes or until firm. Leave to cool in the tin, then turn out and store in an airtight tin or wrapped in foil for 3 days before eating. Dredge heavily with sifted icing sugar before serving.

TO FREEZE: *Wrap tightly in foil. Keeps for 4 months.*

Apricot, Caraway
and Brandy Ring

*A Polish friend makes this cake every Christmas, and I must admit
it makes a light contrast to all the richer cakes around.*

- 225 G/8 OZ NO-NEED-TO-SOAK DRIED APRICOTS, ROUGHLY CHOPPED
- 100 G/4 OZ SULTANAS
- 4 TBSP RUM OR BRANDY
- 150 ML/¼ PINT FRESH ORANGE JUICE
- 175 G/6 OZ SELF-RAISING FLOUR
- 1 TSP BAKING POWDER
- 175 G/6 OZ BUTTER, AT ROOM TEMPERATURE
- 5 TBSP CLEAR HONEY
- 4 EGGS, SIZE 3, SEPARATED
- 1 TSP CARAWAY SEEDS
- TOPPING (OPTIONAL, SEE STEP 5)

1 Place the apricot and sultanas in a saucepan with the rum or brandy and the orange juice. Bring to the boil, stirring all the time, then remove from the heat and leave to cool and soak for 2–3 hours.

2 Set the oven to 180°C/350°F/Gas 4. Grease a 1.2 litre/2 pint ring mould.

3 Sift the flour and baking powder together. Beat the butter and honey together until light and fluffy. Beat in the egg yolks, adding a little flour to prevent curdling, then gently fold in the cooled apricot mixture, the remaining flour and the caraway seeds. Whisk the egg whites until they form soft peaks, then fold into the mixture as gently as possible.

4 Spoon into the mould and spread the top level. Bake for about 1¼ hours or until a skewer inserted into the deepest part comes out clean. Leave to cool in the mould for 10 minutes, then turn out on to a wire rack to cool completely. For an even boozier cake, sprinkle with more rum or brandy whilst still warm.

5 Serve plain, or paint with apricot glaze (see page 169) and sprinkle with golden granulated sugar, or decorate with glacé and crystallized fruits. Or drizzle glacé icing (see page 166) over the top and sides and top with a ring of chopped dried apricots.

TO FREEZE: *Wrap undecorated cake in foil. Keeps for 4 months.*

Illustrated opposite page 64

$\mathcal{G}$INGERBREAD

*This gingerbread is made by the melting method, and is an easy cake
for children to bake.*

- 350 G/12 OZ SELF-RAISING
  FLOUR
- PINCH SALT
- 2 TSP GROUND GINGER
- 2 TSP GROUND CINNAMON
- 175 G/6 OZ BUTTER OR
  BLOCK MARGARINE
- 2 ROUNDED TBSP GOLDEN SYRUP
- 2 ROUNDED TBSP DARK
  TREACLE

- 175 G/6 OZ DARK MUSCOVADO
  SUGAR
- 2 EGGS, SIZE 3
- 150 ML/¼ PINT MILK
- **CINNAMON GLACÉ ICING**
  (OPTIONAL):
- 225 G/8 OZ ICING SUGAR
- ¼ TSP GROUND CINNAMON
- FRESHLY SQUEEZED
  ORANGE JUICE, TO MIX

1 Set the oven to 180°C/350°F/Gas 4. Grease and line a 20cm/8inch square cake tin.

2 Sift the flour, salt and spices into a bowl. Place the fat, syrup, treacle and sugar in
a saucepan, or in the microwave oven, and heat until the fat melts. Stir together, then
cool slightly.

3 Pour the melted mixture into the flour, then beat in the eggs and milk. Pour into
the prepared tin. Bake for about 1¼ hours or until firm in the centre. Leave to cool
in the tin, then turn out and store for 1–2 days before eating. The longer the cake is
kept, the stickier it becomes.

4 If liked, cover with cinnamon glacé icing: sift the icing sugar with the ground
cinnamon. Blend to a coating consistency with freshly squeezed orange juice.

TO FREEZE: *Wrap in foil. Keeps for 3 months.*

LITTLE CAKES

CHAPTER FOUR

Morning coffee or afternoon tea parties are excellent ways to entertain friends and neighbours, and don't involve a lot of expense. A simple way to celebrate a birthday or christening is to make a good selection of small cakes and sandwiches, which is so much easier than a large scale buffet.

Little cakes can look stunning arranged on a stylish cloth with the best china. You can bake some of them well ahead of time and freeze them, decorating on the day, and mix in a few freshly made ones. A good selection of meringues, slices, fancies and scones will tempt even the strongest willed, and you will actually have far more time to chat with your guests, when you don't have to worry about cooking hot food. I think we should all make an effort to resurrect the tea party as it is really one of the most civilized and relaxing ways to entertain.

LITTLE CAKES

$\mathcal{E}$NGLISH MADELEINES

MAKES 12

These are a classic feature of the English tea table.

- 1 QUANTITY EASY CUPCAKES
  MIXTURE (SEE PAGE 82)
- 6 TBSP RASPBERRY JAM
- JUICE ½ LEMON

- 50 G/2 OZ DESICCATED
  COCONUT
- 6 GLACÉ CHERRIES, HALVED

1 Set the oven to 190°C/375°F/Gas 5. Grease 12 dariole moulds well and line the base of each with a small disc of greaseproof paper.

2 Divide the cupcakes mixture among the moulds. Bake for 15–20 minutes. Cool in the moulds for a few minutes, then turn out on to a wire rack to cool. When cold, trim the bases so that the cakes stand up straight.

3 Heat the jam and lemon juice in a small pan, or the microwave oven, until the jam melts. Pour through a sieve to remove the pips.

4 Hold each cake on a fork, and brush with the warm jam mixture. Place the coconut on a plate and roll each madeleine in it to cover top and sides evenly. Place each cake in a paper case, and decorate each with a halved cherry.

TO FREEZE: *Pack undecorated cakes in a rigid container. Keeps for 3 months.*

Illustrated opposite page 80

*Roll madeleines into jam
then grated coconut*

*Top with halved cherries
and angelica leaves*

$\mathscr{F}$RENCH MADELEINES

Marcel Proust ate madeleines with lime blossom tea as a child, when visiting his aunt on Sunday mornings. Ever since he wrote about these dainty little cakes in Remembrance of Things Past, *they have had a mystique which makes them very special, if not slightly formal. Madeleines will keep for up to a week in an airtight tin.*

- 50 G/2 OZ UNSALTED BUTTER
- 2 EGGS, SIZE 3

- 50 G/2 OZ CASTER SUGAR, STORED WITH A VANILLA POD
- 50 G/2 OZ PLAIN FLOUR

Fill moulds three-quarters full

1 Set the oven to 200°C/400°F/Gas 6. Lightly grease two sheets of scalloped madeleine moulds with melted butter. Dust with flour, then tap away any excess.

2 Melt the butter, then remove from heat and allow to cool. Place the eggs and sugar in a heatproof bowl set over a pan of hot water and whisk until the mixture is very thick and pale and firm enough to leave a ribbon trail when the whisk is lifted. Remove from the heat and continue whisking for 2 minutes.

3 Sift the flour over the surface and fold in very gently with a metal spoon. Fold in the lukewarm butter. Fill each of the moulds three-quarters full and level them. Bake for about 10–14 minutes until firm and pale golden. Cool in the tins for 1 minute, then turn out on to a wire rack and leave to cool completely.

TO FREEZE: *Layer in a rigid container, interleaved with freezer tissue. Keeps for 3 months.*

Illustrated opposite page 80

NAPOLEONS

MAKES 12

Definitely very fancy work for a special occasion, but the pastry layers and cream can both be prepared well in advance and assembled on the day.

- 225 G/8 OZ PUFF PASTRY, PREFERABLY LAYERED SHEET TYPE
- **ALMOND CREAM FILLING:**
- 110 G/4 OZ SACHET POWDERED GELATINE
- 450 ML/3/4 PINT MILK
- 25 G/1 OZ CORNFLOUR
- 50 G/2 OZ CASTER SUGAR, STORED WITH A VANILLA POD
- 2 EGGS, SIZE 3, BEATEN

- 1 TSP ALMOND ESSENCE
- 150 ML/1/4 PINT WHIPPING CREAM
- **DECORATION:**
- 75 G/3 OZ PLAIN CHOCOLATE
- 350 G/12 OZ ICING SUGAR, SIFTED
- 2 TBSP GOLDEN SYRUP
- 1/4 TSP VANILLA ESSENCE
- 1 TSP WHITE VEGETABLE FAT

1 Make the filling first. Sprinkle the gelatine over 4 tbsp of the milk and leave to soften. Blend the cornflour and sugar to a smooth paste with 2 tbsp milk in a saucepan, then blend in the rest of the milk. Bring to the boil, stirring constantly, and cook for 1 minute until thick. Remove from the heat and quickly beat in the eggs. Heat gently so that the eggs thicken the custard, then remove from the heat again and stir in the gelatine and essence. Stir until the gelatine is completely dissolved, then leave to cool and begin to set.

2 Cut the pastry into four quarters, or use four separate thin sheets if possible. Roll each piece to a rectangle 20 × 25cm/8 × 10inches, and place each piece on a wetted baking sheet. Chill for 30 minutes.

3 Set the oven to 200°C/400°F/Gas 6. Prick the pastry all over with a fork and bake two sheets at a time for 15–20 minutes until well risen and golden. Place on wire racks to cool.

4 Whip the cream until it forms soft peaks, and gently fold into the setting custard mixture. Chill until firm.

5 Trim all the pastry layers to the same size using a sharp knife. Choose the best and flattest layer for the top.

6 To make the decoration, melt the chocolate in a small heatproof bowl set over a pan of warm water or in the microwave oven. Put aside. Place the icing sugar, syrup, 2 tbsp water, the vanilla essence and fat in a heatproof bowl over a pan of hot water and heat gently, stirring, until the mixture is smooth and shiny and coats the back of the spoon. Do not allow to boil. If the icing is too thick add a little more water.

7 Place the melted chocolate in a paper piping bag (see page 182) and snip off the tip. Pour the icing directly from the bowl over the top pastry layer and spread even. Pipe strips of melted chocolate, 2.5cm/1inch apart, lengthways down the icing. Feather by pulling a skewer through the chocolate at 1cm/½inch intervals, crossways. Leave the icing and chocolate to set.

8 When the almond cream filling is firm, spread one-third over a plain pastry layer. Place on a serving plate and set another plain pastry layer on top. Layer with the remaining filling and pastry, finishing with the iced layer on top. Chill for 30 minutes, during which time the pastry will sink a little.

9 To serve, cut down the centre lengthways with a very sharp knife, then cut each half crossways into six thin fingers.

Not suitable for freezing.

Illustrated opposite page 128

Cut sponge into small shapes

Pour over boiled fondant icing
and stand on a rack to set

Decorate with fondant
flowers, cherries and nuts

FONDANT FANCIES

MAKES ABOUT 12

Fancies are made from one layer of sponge. Use patterned cutters
for interesting shapes.

100 G/4 OZ SELF-RAISING
FLOUR
PINCH SALT
25 G/1 OZ CORNFLOUR
100 G/4 OZ BUTTER OR
BLOCK MARGARINE,
AT ROOM TEMPERATURE
100 G/4 OZ CASTER SUGAR

FINELY GRATED ZEST ½ LEMON
2 EGGS, SIZE 2, BEATEN
1–2 TBSP MILK
TO FINISH:
APRICOT JAM, SIEVED
BOILED FONDANT ICING
(SEE PAGE 164)

1 Set the oven to 190°C/375°F/Gas 5. Grease and line a 28 × 18cm/11 × 7inch baking tin.

2 Sift the flour, salt and cornflour together. Cream the fat, sugar and zest together until light and fluffy. Gradually beat in the eggs, adding a little flour with each addition. Fold in the remaining flour with a large metal spoon and add enough milk to give a smooth consistency.

3 Spoon into the tin and spread level. Bake in the centre of the oven for about 20 minutes or until firm and golden. Cool in the tin for 3 minutes then turn out on to a wire rack to cool.

4 Cut into 12 squares, or other shapes using small cutters. Brush each square with sieved apricot jam and pour over boiled fondant icing. Decorate with crystallized flowers, fondant icing flowers (see pages 179–81) or shapes, or halved glacé cherries, walnuts and angelica. Serve in paper cases.

TO FREEZE: *Wrap undecorated, uncut slab cake in foil. Keeps for 3 months.*

Illustrated opposite page 80

SCOTTISH SHORTBREAD

*Being married to a Scot, I always make plenty of shortbread,
especially for New Year's Eve. This recipe makes enough for two
rounds, so you can give one to a friend as a New Year's present,
with a piece of coal and a wee dram, of course. The shortbread will
keep well in an airtight tin for up to 2 weeks.*

- 275 G/10 OZ PLAIN FLOUR
- 50 G/2 OZ RICE FLOUR
- PINCH SALT
- 75 G/3 OZ CASTER SUGAR
- 250 G/9 OZ BUTTER, AT ROOM TEMPERATURE
- CASTER SUGAR, TO DREDGE

1 Set the oven to 160°C/325°F/Gas 3. Grease two baking sheets.

2 Sift the flours and salt into a bowl and stir in the caster sugar. Add the butter cut into small pieces and rub into the dry ingredients until the mixture resembles crumbs. You will then find that it can be kneaded into a soft dough, using no liquid.

3 Knead until a smooth ball is formed. Cut it in half and roll out each piecce into a 20cm/8inch round. Mark into eight wedges, and flute the edges like pastry, then prick with a fork.

*Mark into eight wedges
and flute edges*

4 Place a round on each baking sheet. Bake for about 35–40 minutes or until pale golden. Leave to cool completely on the sheets, as the warm shortbread is very soft to handle.

5 Dust with caster sugar, and tie up with red ribbons.

TO FREEZE: *Wrap in foil. Keeps for 2 months.*

Illustrated opposite page 97

CHOUX PASTRY SWANS

MAKES 8

*These choux pastry swans are fun to make for tea,
or for a surprise dinner party pudding.*

- CHOUX PASTRY:
- 100 G/4 OZ STRONG PLAIN FLOUR
- 2 TSP CASTER SUGAR
- PINCH SALT
- 75 G/3 OZ BUTTER

- 225 ML/8 FL OZ WATER
- 3 EGGS, SIZE 3
- **TO FINISH:**
- 300 ML/½ PINT DOUBLE OR WHIPPING CREAM
- ICING SUGAR, TO DREDGE

1 Set the oven to 200°C/400°F/Gas 6. Grease two baking sheets, then dust lightly with flour. Using your finger, trace eight figure '2's about 7.5cm/3inches high and eight oval shapes 7.5cm/3inches long on the baking sheets.

2 Sift the flour, sugar and salt on to a stiff piece of paper (you need to do this in order to add the flour all at once). Place the butter in a heavy-based saucepan with the water and heat until the butter melts, then bring to the boil. Shoot in the flour all at once and beat the mixture well with a wooden spoon until it leaves the sides of the pan and forms a ball. Take off the heat and cool for a minute, then beat in the eggs, using an electric mixer if possible. Beat until the mixture is smooth and glossy.

3 Spoon the choux pastry into a piping bag fitted with a 1cm/½inch plain nozzle. Pipe carefully on to the '2' shapes and into the ovals. Bake for about 15 minutes or until well risen and crisp, then make a small hole in each oval to allow the steam to escape. Return to the oven for another 3 minutes to dry out the pastry. Cool on wire racks.

4 To finish, whip the cream until stiff, adding a little liqueur or sugar to sweeten if liked. Cut each oval in half horizontally, then cut the top half in half lengthways to form two wings. Place some cream in the bottom half of each and press a '2' into this for the swan's neck. Press the two halves into the cream at an angle to form the wings. Lightly dust the wings with sifted icing sugar. Serve immediately, as the cream will start to soften the pastry if left too long.

Not suitable for freezing.

*Pipe ovals and '2' shapes
of choux pastry*

*Split ovals when baked,
then cut tops into halves*

*Assemble swans, securing
pieces with cream*

RIGHT (from top to bottom): Choux Pastry Swans (see above); English Madeleines (see page 74); French Madeleines (see page 75); Fondant Fancies (see page 78).

$\mathcal{V}$IENNESE WHIRLS

MAKES 10–12

These little cakes are easy to make and are a good contrast to the richer items on the tea table.

- 175 G/6 OZ BUTTER OR BLOCK MARGARINE, AT ROOM TEMPERATURE
- 175 G/6 OZ PLAIN FLOUR
- 75 G/3 OZ CASTER SUGAR
- FEW DROPS VANILLA ESSENCE
- ICING SUGAR, TO DREDGE
- **TO FINISH:**
- 2–3 TBSP SIEVED RASPBERRY JAM

1 Set the oven to 180°C/350°F/Gas 4. Place twelve paper baking cases in a deep-hole bun tray.

2 Beat the fat until very soft and fluffy, then sift in the flour and beat in gradually. Beat in the sugar and vanilla essence. Spoon into a large piping bag fitted with a medium star nozzle.

3 Pipe into a rosette in each paper case. Bake in the centre of the oven for about 20 minutes or until light golden in colour. Leave to cool, in the paper cases, on a wire rack.

4 Dust with sifted icing sugar when cold, and fill the centre of each with a spot of raspberry jam.

TO FREEZE: *Freeze unbaked mixture in paper cases in a rigid container. Keeps for 6 weeks. Thaw at room temperature and bake as above.*

Illustrated opposite page 81

LEFT (from top to bottom): Bakewell Tart Tray Bake (see page 88); Paradise Slices (see page 86); Viennese Whirls (see above); Chocolate Dipped Golden Meringues (see page 84).

EASY CUPCAKES

There are endless decorating possibilities with these simple little cakes. Enlist the help of children for some new ideas.

- 100 G/4 OZ BUTTER OR BLOCK MARGARINE, AT ROOM TEMPERATURE
- 100 G/4 OZ CASTER SUGAR
- 2 EGGS, SIZE 3, BEATEN

- 150 G/5 OZ SELF-RAISING FLOUR
- FEW DROPS VANILLA ESSENCE
- 1–2 TBSP MILK
- TOPPING (SEE STEP 4)

1 Set the oven to 190°C/375°F/Gas 5. Arrange 18–20 paper baking cases in deep-hole bun trays.

2 Cream the fat and sugar together until light and fluffy, then beat in the eggs a little at a time, adding a teaspoon of flour with each addition. Gently fold in the remaining flour. Add the vanilla essence to the milk and fold in enough to give a soft consistency.

3 Spoon the mixture into the paper cases, filling them about two-thirds full. Bake for about 15 minutes or until well risen, firm and golden. Cool, in the paper cases, on a wire rack.

4 Decorate with glacé icing (see page 166), or with simple buttercream (see page 170), made using 75g/3oz unsalted butter and 175g/6oz icing sugar. If liked, divide the buttercream into portions and colour each differently, then use a piping bag with a small star nozzle to pipe patterns and shapes on top of each cupcake. Make butterfly wings by cutting away the centre top of each cake and cutting this in half. Position as 'wings', securing with a little buttercream, and pipe buttercream down the centre for the butterfly body.

TO FREEZE: *Freeze undecorated in rigid polythene boxes. Keeps for 2 months.*

Illustrated opposite page 17

$\mathcal{M}$ACAROONS

MAKES 20–24

A great Scottish favourite, home-made macaroons are hard to beat.
Make them larger for tea-time, or tiny as after-dinner petits fours.

- 100 G/4 OZ GROUND ALMONDS
- 175 G/6 OZ CASTER SUGAR
- 2 EGG WHITES, SIZE 3
- FEW DROPS ALMOND ESSENCE

- EGG WHITE TO GLAZE
- CASTER SUGAR, TO SPRINKLE
- 20–24 ALMOND HALVES

1 Set the oven to 180°C/350°F/Gas 4. Line two baking sheets with rice paper.

2 Mix the almonds and sugar together in a bowl. Whisk the egg whites with the almond essence in another bowl until stiff. Gradually beat in the almonds and sugar until the mixture forms a fairly stiff paste. Spoon into a large piping bag fitted with a 1cm/½inch nozzle.

3 Pipe out 20–24 small rounds, spaced well apart, on the rice paper. Brush each one lightly with egg white and sprinkle very lightly with caster sugar. Press a halved almond into each.

4 Bake for 15 minutes or until just beginning to colour. Cool on the sheets until firm, then pull the rice paper apart to separate the cakes.

Not suitable for freezing.

Illustrated opposite page 96

Chocolate Dipped
Golden Meringues

MAKES 12

*These add style to the tea table, and make a good contrast when
mixed into a selection of cakes. The meringues can be made well
ahead of time, and stored in an airtight tin.*

- 75 G/3 OZ GOLDEN CASTER OR
  SOFT LIGHT BROWN SUGAR
- 75 G/3 OZ CASTER SUGAR
- 3 EGG WHITES, SIZE 3
- PINCH CREAM OF TARTAR
- **FILLING:**
- 225 G/8 OZ PLAIN CHOCOLATE

- 150 ML/¼ PINT DOUBLE
  OR WHIPPING CREAM
- 1 PASSION FRUIT, OR
  1 TBSP SPIRIT OR LIQUEUR
  SUCH AS BRANDY, GRAND
  MARNIER OR TIA MARIA

1 Set the oven to 110°C/225°F/Gas ¼. Line two baking sheets with some non-stick
silicone paper.

2 Sift the sugars together. Place the egg whites in a completely grease-free bowl and
whisk with the cream of tartar until they are stiff and standing in peaks. Whisk in the
sugars, a tablespoon at a time, making sure the meringue is stiff before adding the
next addition.

3 Place the meringue in a piping bag fitted with a small plain nozzle. Pipe out 24
small rounds on to the non-stick paper. Bake for about 1½ hours or until crisp and
dry, reversing the trays in the oven halfway through the cooking. Leave to cool on the
paper, then peel off the meringues and store in an airtight tin until needed.

4 To finish, break up the chocolate and melt very gently in a heatproof bowl set
over a pan of warm water or in the microwave oven. Paint the flat underside of each
meringue lightly with a layer of melted chocolate and leave to dry.

5 Whip the cream until stiff. Halve the passion fruit and scoop out the flesh into a
sieve. Press the passion fruit juice through the sieve over the cream bowl, leaving the
pips in the sieve. Fold the juice (or liqueur) into the cream, then use to sandwich pairs
of meringues together, chocolate sides in. Place in paper cases to serve.

Not suitable for freezing.

Illustrated opposite page 81

$\mathcal{R}$UNNING A STALL
FOR CHARITY

If you have a reputation for good home baking you may well find yourself 'volunteered' to run a cake stall for a local charity. This really can be fun and very rewarding if you have a good military plan of attack. The following tactics will help you on your way.

☞ Make lots of different bakes in small batches as a variety of cakes always looks more attractive, and gives more choice. Bake and freeze over a few weeks, or ask two or three friends to make one batch each to help.

☞ Cost out all recipes before you bake. Try to keep the prices as low as possible, then people will buy two or three items.

☞ Start collecting chocolate boxes and attractive packaging well in advance. Package everything invitingly with doilies and ribbons; for fragile items, cover boxes with wrapping paper and top with cellophane.

☞ Label clearly so that people know what they are buying, including price, storage, and freezing instructions (but only if the cakes are fresh).

☞ Have plenty of paper and carrier bags for purchases to be taken away in.

☞ Start with plenty of change in your cash box, as lack of it can hinder sales.

☞ Make your stall and helpers as attractive as possible. Wear spotlessly clean matching aprons if possible to give a professional image.

The cakes on the following pages are good for selling at charity events as they can be made up in bulk and cut up on the day of the fête. Try two or three varieties.

$\mathcal{C}$HINESE CHEWS

MAKES 16 SLICES

Not as chewy as the name suggests, but sticky and delicious.

- 225 G/8 OZ STONED DATES, CHOPPED
- 100 G/4 OZ WALNUT PIECES, CHOPPED
- 200 G/7 OZ DARK MUSCOVADO SUGAR

- 75 G/3 OZ PLAIN FLOUR
- 1 TSP BAKING POWDER
- 3 EGGS, SIZE 3, BEATEN

1 Set the oven to 180°C/350°F/Gas 4. Grease and line an 18 × 28cm/7 × 11inch tin.

2 Mix all the ingredients together, then pour into the tin and spread evenly. Bake just above the centre of the oven for about 25 minutes. Leave to cool in the tin, and mark into squares or fingers whilst still warm. Cut when cold.

TO FREEZE: *Wrap in foil. Keeps for 2 months.*

TREACLE SCONES

MAKES 12

*These are a Scottish favourite for tea-time. Just a wee bit different
from plain scones, these are delicious split and buttered.*

- 225 G/8 OZ PLAIN FLOUR
- ½ TSP BICARBONATE OF SODA
- 1 TSP CREAM OF TARTAR
- ½ TSP SALT
- ½ TSP GROUND CINNAMON

- ½ TSP MIXED SPICE
- 25 G/1 OZ BUTTER
- 25 G/1 OZ CASTER SUGAR
- 1 TBSP TREACLE
- 150 ML/¼ PT MILK, TO MIX

1 Set the oven to 230°C/450°F/Gas 8. Grease a baking sheet.

2 Sift the dry ingredients into a bowl and rub in the butter until the mixture
resembles fine crumbs. Stir in the sugar. Dilute the treacle with a little milk, then add
to the mixture and mix to a light dough, adding more milk as necessary.

3 Turn out on to a floured surface and knead lightly until smooth. Roll out to about
2cm/¾inch thick and cut into rounds using a 5cm/2inch floured cutter, cutting as
close to each other as possible. Re-roll the trimmings and make more rounds.

4 Place on the baking sheet. Bake for about 10 minutes or until well risen. Serve hot
or cold, split and buttered.

TO FREEZE: *Wrap in freezer bags or store in rigid container. Keeps for up to 6 months.*

PARADISE SLICES

MAKES 16 SLICES

*These are lovely old-fashioned cakes, with a homely quality. Keep
some handy in the cake tin, or freezer.*

- 225 G/8 OZ SHORTCRUST PASTRY
- 100 G/4 OZ SOFT TUB
  MARGARINE
- 100 G/4 OZ CASTER SUGAR
- 2 EGGS, SIZE 3
- 50 G/2 OZ GROUND ALMONDS
- 50 G/2 OZ SELF-RAISING FLOUR

- 3–4 TBSP JAM OR MARMALADE
- 25 G/1 OZ SULTANAS
- 25 G/1 OZ CURRANTS
- 25 G/1 OZ GLACÉ CHERRIES,
  RINSED, DRIED AND QUARTERED
- ICING SUGAR, TO DREDGE

1 Set the oven to 200°C/400°F/Gas 6. Grease an 18 × 28cm/7 × 11inch tin.

2 Roll out the pastry and use to line the tin. Cover with greaseproof paper and weigh down with baking beans. Bake blind for 15 minutes or until the pastry is light golden. Remove the paper and beans. Turn the oven down to 180°C/350°F/Gas 4.

3 Beat the margarine, sugar, eggs, almonds and flour together quickly until smooth. Spread the jam in the pastry case, then sprinkle over the dried fruit and cherries evenly. Spread the sponge mixture over the top.

4 Bake for about 20 minutes or until the sponge is firm in the centre. Leave to cool in the tin. Dredge with sifted icing or caster sugar when cold and cut into slices.

TO FREEZE: *Freeze in baking tin, covered with foil. Keeps for 2 months.*

Illustrated opposite page 81

ℬAKLAVA

MAKES 20

Filo or strudel pastry is now available from supermarkets, so it is easy to make this rich Middle Eastern delicacy.

- 225 G/8 OZ CHOPPED MIXED NUTS OR WALNUTS
- 50 G/2 OZ CASTER SUGAR
- ½ TSP GROUND CINNAMON
- 450 G/1 LB FILO PASTRY

- 175 G/6 OZ BUTTER, MELTED
- 175 G/6 OZ CLEAR HONEY
- 50 G/2 OZ SHELLED PISTACHIO NUTS, FINELY CHOPPED (OPTIONAL)

1 Set the oven to 220°C/425°F/Gas 7. Butter a 23 × 18cm/9 × 7inch tin.

2 Chop or process the nuts until fairly fine, then mix with the sugar and spice.

3 Cut the sheets of pastry to measure 25cm/10inches square. Fit one square into the tin, then brush with melted butter. Repeat with five more buttered layers of pastry, then sprinkle over 50g/2oz of the nut mixture.

4 Repeat the last stage four more times to give five layers of nut mixture. Top with the remaining pastry, then trim the pastry edges. Using a very sharp knife, mark the pastry into 20 squares.

5 Bake for 10 minutes, then lower the oven temperature to 180°C/350°F/Gas 4 and bake for about 15 minutes longer or until golden.

6 Heat the honey in a small pan or in the microwave until melted, then pour over the cooked pastry. Leave to cool in the tin for 2–3 hours, then cut through the squares again. Sprinkle the top with chopped pistachio nuts to decorate.

Not suitable for freezing.

Illustrated opposite page 17

$\mathscr{B}$AKEWELL TART
TRAY BAKE

<u>MAKES 16 SLICES</u>

This is a good recipe to bake up for bazaars, as the almonds keep the filling moist, and you can make the bakewell tart the day before, or freeze it well in advance.

PASTRY:
75 G/3 OZ BLOCK MARGARINE
175 G/6 OZ PLAIN FLOUR
ICING SUGAR, TO DREDGE
TOPPING:
3–4 TBSP SEEDLESS
RASPBERRY JAM
150 G/5 OZ SOFT TUB
MARGARINE
75 G/3 OZ CASTER SUGAR

2 EGGS, SIZE 2, BEATEN
¼ TSP ALMOND ESSENCE
100 G/4 OZ GROUND ALMONDS
50 G/2 OZ SELF-RAISING FLOUR
2 TBSP MILK
50 G/2 OZ FLAKED ALMONDS
TO FINISH:
ICING SUGAR, TO DREDGE,
OR GLACÉ ICING (PAGE 166)

1 Set the oven to 200°C/400°F/Gas 6. Grease an 18 × 28cm/7 × 11inch shallow baking tin or roasting tray.

2 To make the pastry, rub the margarine into the flour until it resembles fine crumbs, then stir in enough cold water to bind to a soft dough. Knead lightly, then roll out and use to line the baking tin. Prick lightly all over with a fork. Spread with the raspberry jam, and chill while making the topping.

3 Place all the remaining topping ingredients, except the flaked almonds, in a bowl and quickly beat together until smooth. Spread over the jam and level the top. Sprinkle with the flaked almonds.

4 Bake just above the centre of the oven until golden and springy to the touch in the centre. Leave to cool in the tin, then turn out and dredge heavily with sifted icing sugar. Alternatively, drizzle over glacé icing. Cut into 16 slices.

VARIATIONS: *Use 4 tbsp mincemeat or marmalade instead of traditional raspberry jam.*

TO FREEZE: *Wrap in freezer bags. Keeps for 3 months.*

Illustrated opposite page 81

MOCHA NUT SQUARES

MAKES 18

These are easy to bake for sale or bazaars. Make them in bulk in a large tin, spread over the icing, and simply cut into squares — couldn't be easier.

- 175 G/6 OZ SOFT TUB MARGARINE
- 50 G/2 OZ SHELLED WALNUTS, CHOPPED
- 175 G/6 OZ SOFT LIGHT BROWN SUGAR
- 3 EGGS, SIZE 3, BEATEN
- 1 TBSP COFFEE ESSENCE, OR 1 TBSP INSTANT COFFEE DISSOLVED IN 1 TBSP BOILING WATER

- 175 G/6 OZ SELF-RAISING FLOUR
- 1½ TSP BAKING POWDER
- **MOCHA ICING:**
- 225 G/8 OZ ICING SUGAR
- 75 G/3 OZ SOFT TUB MARGARINE
- 1 TBSP COCOA POWDER
- 2 TSP INSTANT COFFEE POWDER
- 1 TBSP MILK

1 Grease and base-line a 30 × 22 × 5cm/12 × 8 × 2inch tin. Set the oven to 180°C/350°F/Gas 4.

2 Place the margarine, walnuts, sugar, eggs and coffee essence in a bowl. Sift in the flour and baking powder and quickly beat together until smooth.

3 Spread in the tin and smooth level. Bake for 35 minutes or until the sides begin to shrink away from the tin and the centre is springy. Leave to cool in the tin for 10 minutes, then turn out on to a wire rack and peel away the lining paper.

4 To make the icing, sift the icing sugar into a bowl and add the margarine. Blend the cocoa and coffee with 1 tbsp boiling water. Cool a little, then stir in to the sugar with the milk. Beat until smooth.

5 Spread the icing over the top of the cold cake and, if liked, sprinkle with chopped walnuts. Cut into 3 lengthways, then cut into 18 squares.

TO FREEZE: *Wrap un-iced cake in foil. Keeps for 3 months.*

Illustrated opposite page 17

$\mathcal{R}$ ICH AND
LIGHT FRUIT CAKES

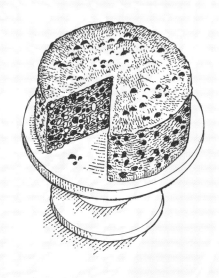

*F*ruits have been dried from very early times, and in Arab cuisine formed part of the staple winter diet. Little cakes stuffed with rich fruit fillings were, and still are, made in this part of the world. In Europe, the first fruit cakes were simple bread doughs enriched with spice and dried fruits, and the cakes we bake today have evolved from these.

Rich fruit cakes were often symbols of prosperity and fertility in the past and are still the traditional centrepieces for all kinds of family celebrations like weddings, christenings and Christmas.

As well as the beautifully decorated centrepieces for grand occasions, fruit cakes can be perfect to bake and keep in the tin for tea. Sliced and buttered there is nothing that can beat a piece of tasty fruit cake with a cup of tea to revive flagging spirits and help you through the day.

RICH AND
LIGHT FRUIT
CAKES

$\mathcal{F}$RUIT CAKE INGREDIENTS

BUTTER

Most rich fruit cakes are made by creaming the butter, and this is a vital stage, which must be done thoroughly to give a light fluffy mixture; air gives the cake its structure. Large amounts of butter are more easily beaten in a free-standing table-top mixer, as hand-held mixers can become overheated with the strain. Alternatively, you can beat by hand – try small batches if the mix is large or you will soon become tired. Use salted butter in rich cakes, for a good flavour. When I trained at Westminster College, we had to beat the very yellow salted New Zealand butter by hand until it turned pale. Although this was hard work, I've not found a better basis for a cake yet.

SUGAR

Moist dark brown sugar is essential for rich cakes. Muscovado and molasses are relatively unrefined raw sugars which give wonderful flavour and colour, and are well worth using. If brown sugar from your store-cupboard has dried and gone hard, place it in a bowl, cover with a damp cloth or slices of bread, and leave overnight.

DRIED FRUIT

Most vine fruits such as currants, sultanas and raisins are sold ready cleaned and washed, but it is still advisable to pick them over, as stalks, stems and small stones can escape the factory cleaning, especially in the cheaper brands. You really do get what you pay for with dried fruits, so don't skimp at this stage.

Plump up weighed-out fruit before mixing – steep it in warm water for 15–30 minutes, then spread out on a tea towel or kitchen paper to soak up excess liquid, or steep in sherry, rum or brandy for 3–5 days prior to baking, stirring daily. West Indian cooks soak their fruit in dark rum, brandy, port and cherry brandy for months in sealed jars, which gives the most delicious flavour ever!

TINS

Cake tins for rich, heavy cakes need to be deep, firm and of good quality. All sorts of shapes and sizes like hearts, hexagons, ovals and petals can now be bought or hired. To find the capacity of a shaped tin, fill a 20cm/8inch round tin with water to the baking level. Pour into the shaped tin, noting the amount, and adapt from the chart (see page 97) accordingly.

Make sure that all tins, especially square ones, have sharp corners, not curved ones, as these are difficult to cover with marzipan. Some very old tins can measure smaller in size and newer ones can actually be larger by 5mm/¼inch, so bear this in mind when timing the baking.

DEPTH TEST

If you are making a tiered cake, make sure that all the tins are filled to exactly the same depth. Check by inserting a skewer marked with the exact level into each tin; you can then even them out if they are not the same. When baking a three-tiered cake, you can cook two or three tiers in the same oven, but rotate their shelf positions halfway through the baking time, moving the largest cake to the highest position. Opening the door for such a short period will not do any harm. When baking more than one cake at a time the total cooking time will be a little longer. Do not be tempted to raise the temperature to speed things up or a tough outer crust will form.

Press a hollow into centre

of cake mixture

RICH FRUIT CAKE

*This cake is suitable for a Christmas, wedding or formal
celebration. It is moist and fruity and gets better with keeping, so do
try to make it well ahead of time. For the larger cakes on the chart it
might be easier to make up the mixture the day before, as they do
need long slow cooking. The mixture will not be harmed from being
left overnight. Just put it in the tins, cover with a sheet of paper,
and leave in a cool place until needed.*

1 Set the oven to 150°C/300°F/Gas 2. Grease and line the tin(s), using a treble thickness of greaseproof paper. Tie a double thickness of newspaper or brown paper round the outside of the tin to help protect the sides of the cake from forming a hard crust.

2 Place the butter and sugar in a warmed mixing bowl and cream until very light and fluffy. This can be quite hard work, especially if it is a very large cake, but it is vital to cream the mixture well, to provide a structure for the rest of the ingredients.

3 Add the eggs in small batches, beating well between each addition. Add a teaspoon of flour if the mixture begins to curdle. Sift in the flour and spice, then sprinkle over the dried fruit and peel. Fold the mixture together (use your hand for this if you have lots of mixture – it is much easier).

4 Add the cherries, nuts, treacle and brandy and mix well, making sure all the fruit is combined and that there are no patches of flour in the mixture.

5 Turn the mixture into the tin and make a hollow in the centre, to prevent the cake from peaking when it rises. Stand the tin on a double sheet of newspaper or brown paper. Bake for 1 hour, then turn down the oven temperature to 140°C/275°F/Gas 1 for the remaining time. To test the cake, insert a warmed skewer into the centre. If it comes out clean, the cake is cooked; if any sticky mixture adheres to it, bake the cake a little longer.

6 When cooked, leave the cake in the tin to cool. Turn it out, leaving on the lining paper. Prick the top with a fine skewer and paint brandy or rum over the cold cake. (Repeat this process 2 or 3 times during storage for a really rich cake.) Overwrap the cake in sheets of greaseproof paper and tape tightly and neatly. Overwrap the greaseproof paper with doubled foil and tape tightly to make an airtight parcel. Place on a really level surface, or a baking sheet, and store in a cool dry place for 2–3 months.

TO FREEZE: *Rich fruit cakes improve with freezing, which tends to blend and mellow the flavours more quickly. Apart from freezing cut pieces, this is the only real reason for freezing as a rich fruit cake will keep well in a tin for a number of years. Freeze the cake wrapped as above. Keeps for 4 months. Leave plenty of time for thawing, especially for a larger cake.*

Illustrated opposite page 16

$\mathcal{R}$ICH FRUIT CAKES

Round tin	15cm/6inch	18cm/7inch	20cm/8inch	23cm/9inch	25cm/10inch	28cm/11inch	30cm/12inch	
Square tin	12cm/5inch	15cm/6inch	18cm/7inch	20cm/8inch	23cm/9inch	25cm/10inch	28cm/11inch	30cm/12inch
Brown sugar	150g/5oz	175g/6oz	275g/10oz	350g/12oz	500g/1lb2oz	600g/1lb5oz	800g/1¾lb	950g/2lb2oz
Butter	150g/5oz	175g/6oz	275g/10oz	350g/12oz	500g/1lb2oz	600g/1lb5oz	800g/1¾lb	950g/2lb2oz
Eggs, size 3	2–2½	3	5	6	9	11	14	16
Plain flour	175g/6oz	225g/8oz	350g/12oz	450g/1lb	600g/1lb5oz	700g/1½lb	800g/1¾lb	1kg/2lb6oz
Mixed spice	¼ tsp	½ tsp	1 tsp	1 tsp	1½ tsp	2 tsp	2½ tsp	3 tsp
Currants	200g/7oz	275g/10oz	400g/14oz	450g/1lb	550g/1¼lb	800g/1¾lb	975g/2lb5oz	1.2kg/2lb11oz
Sultanas	200g/7oz	275g/10oz	400g/14oz	450g/1lb	550g/1¼lb	800g/1¾lb	975g/2lb5oz	1.2kg/2lb11oz
Raisins	50g/2oz	75g/3oz	100g/4oz	225g/8oz	275g/10oz	350g/12oz	400g/14oz	450g/1lb
Chopped candied peel	50g/2oz	75g/3oz	100g/4oz	175g/6oz	225g/8oz	250g/9oz	275g/10oz	350g/12oz
Glacé cherries	25g/1oz	50g/2oz	50g/2oz	75g/3oz	100g/4oz	175g/6oz	225g/8oz	275g/10oz
Flaked almonds	25g/1oz	50g/2oz	50g/2oz	100g/4oz	100g/4oz	175g/6oz	225g/8oz	275g/10oz
Dark treacle	1 tbsp	1 tbsp	1½ tbsp	2 tbsp	3 tbsp	3½ tbsp	4 tbsp	5 tbsp
Rum or brandy	1 tbsp	1 tbsp	1½ tbsp	2 tbsp	2½ tbsp	3 tbsp	3½ tbsp	4 tbsp
Cooking time	2½ hours	3 hours	5 hours	6–6½ hours	7 hours	7½ hours	8 hours	8½ hours

DUNDEE CAKE

This lighter fruit cake is a favourite of mine. I make it for fêtes, for guessing the weight, and as a present for friends. It looks lovely wrapped in cellophane with a tartan ribbon tied round it.

- 100 G/4 OZ SULTANAS
- 100 G/4 OZ CURRANTS
- 100 G/4 OZ RAISINS
- 50 G/2 OZ CHOPPED CANDIED MIXED PEEL
- 75 G/3 OZ GLACÉ CHERRIES, RINSED, DRIED AND CHOPPED
- 75 G/3 OZ GROUND ALMONDS
- 225 G/8 OZ BUTTER, AT ROOM TEMPERATURE

- 225 G/8 OZ SOFT LIGHT BROWN SUGAR
- FINELY GRATED ZEST 1 LEMON
- 3 EGGS, SIZE 3, BEATEN
- 250 G/9 OZ PLAIN FLOUR
- 1 TSP BAKING POWDER
- 1 TBSP SHERRY OR WATER
- 50 G/2 OZ SHELLED ALMONDS, SKINNED

1 Set the oven to 160°C/325°F/Gas 3. Grease and line an 18cm/7inch round deep cake tin.

2 Mix the dried fruits, peel and cherries in a bowl with the ground almonds, tossing to coat the fruit. Cream the butter, sugar and zest together until light and fluffy, then beat in the eggs gradually. Beat in a teaspoon of flour with each addition of egg to prevent the mixture from curdling.

3 Sift the remaining flour and the baking powder together into the dried fruit mixture. Stir together, then add to the creamed mixture a little at a time, mixing in well. Add the sherry or water. Spoon the mixture into the tin and make a slight hollow in the centre, then spread the sides level. Arrange the almonds neatly over the surface in radiating circles.

4 Bake in the centre of the oven for 2½–3 hours or until a skewer inserted in the centre comes out clean, with no mixture sticking to it.

5 Leave to cool in the tin for 10 minutes, then turn out on to a wire rack to cool completely. If liked, decorate with whole almonds, placed in a circle on top. Store in an airtight tin; the flavour will mature and be better after a week.

TO FREEZE: *Wrap whole cake or slices in foil. Keeps for up to 4 months.*

Illustrated opposite page 144

$\mathcal{T}$WELFTH NIGHT CAKE

*The twelfth night after Christmas marks the end of the celebrations
and is the time for taking down the decorations. It was originally a
night for games, feasting and masques in medieval times, and the
Lord of Misrule, appointed at the beginning of Christmas, held his
final court on that day. The French still keep the medieval custom of
baking a cake containing a dried bean. The person who gets the
slice with the bean is King or Queen for the evening, and is crowned
with a paper crown. He or she is all-powerful and can demand
favours and forfeits from the guests, so make sure you know where
the bean is hidden in the cake!*

- 175 G/6 OZ BUTTER, AT ROOM TEMPERATURE, OR SOFT TUB MARGARINE
- 175 G/6 OZ CASTER SUGAR
- 175 G/6 OZ PLAIN FLOUR
- 1½ TSP BAKING POWDER
- 75 G/3 OZ GROUND ALMONDS
- 6 TBSP EVAPORATED MILK
- 3 EGG WHITES, SIZE 3
- 50 G/2 OZ CRYSTALLIZED GINGER, CHOPPED

- 100 G/4 OZ GLACÉ PINEAPPLE, CHOPPED
- 75 G/3 OZ CHOPPED CANDIED MIXED PEEL
- 75 G/3 OZ GLACÉ CHERRIES, RINSED, DRIED AND HALVED
- 75 G/3 OZ FLAKED ALMONDS
- DRIED BEAN (BROAD, KIDNEY OR HARICOT)
- TOPPING (SEE STEP 4)

1 Set the oven to 160°C/325°F/Gas 3. Grease and line a 20cm/8inch round deep cake tin.

2 Cream the fat and sugar together until light and fluffy. Sift in the flour, baking powder and ground almonds, add the evaporated milk and fold together. Whisk the egg whites until stiff, then fold into the mixture with the fruits and nuts. Press the bean into the mixture.

3 Spoon the mixture into the tin and level the top. Bake for about 1½ hours or until firm to the touch in the centre. Leave to cool in the tin for 5 minutes, then turn out on to a wire rack to cool completely.

4 Decorate the top with a fluted round of almond paste (see page 160), or brush the top of the cake with 3 tbsp sieved apricot jam and press over 100g/4oz crystallized fruits in a pattern.

Not suitable for freezing.

Illustrated opposite page 16

GUINNESS CAKE

Start preparations the day before, as you need to soak the fruit overnight for this moist fruit cake. Keep it for a week in an airtight tin for perfect flavour and texture.

- 175 G/6 OZ RAISINS
- 175 G/6 OZ SULTANAS
- 8 TBSP GUINNESS OR STOUT
- 175 G/6 OZ BUTTER, AT ROOM TEMPERATURE
- 175 G/6 OZ DARK MUSCOVADO SUGAR

- 3 EGGS, SIZE 3, BEATEN
- 225 G/8 OZ PLAIN FLOUR
- 2 TSP MIXED SPICE
- 75 G/3 OZ CHOPPED CANDIED MIXED PEEL
- 75 G/3 OZ CHOPPED MIXED NUTS

1 Place the dried fruit in a large bowl, pour over the Guinness and leave to soak for 12 hours, or overnight.

2 Grease and line an 18cm/7inch round cake tin. Set the oven to 170°C/325°F/Gas 3.

3 Cream the butter and sugar together until light and fluffy. Add the eggs gradually, adding a little flour with each addition. Sift the remaining flour with the spice, and fold into the mixture with the soaked fruit and liquid, the peel and nuts. The mixture should be soft and drop easily from a spoon. If it is a little dry, add 1 tbsp milk or water.

4 Spoon the mixture into the tin and spread level. Bake in the centre of the oven for about 1½ hours or until a skewer inserted into the centre of the cake comes out clean.

5 Leave to cool in the tin for 10 minutes, then turn out on to a wire rack and cool completely. Peel away the lining paper and store in an airtight tin for a week before eating, to improve the flavour. Serve sliced and buttered.

TO FREEZE: *Wrap in foil. Keeps for 4 months.*

Illustrated opposite page 97

$\mathcal{B}$LACK BUN

Black bun is an unusual pastry-wrapped cake made in Scotland for the Christmas and New Year celebrations. Scottish children go 'guising' where they soot their faces and sing New Year's songs in exchange for 'hogmanays' – drinks, or gifts of food like black bun.

- 350 G/12 OZ SHORTCRUST PASTRY
- 225 G/8 OZ PLAIN FLOUR
- 1 TSP GROUND CINNAMON
- 1 TSP GROUND GINGER
- 1 TSP GROUND ALLSPICE
- ¼ TSP FRESHLY MILLED BLACK PEPPER
- 1 TSP CREAM OF TARTAR

- 1 TSP BICARBONATE OF SODA
- 900 G/2LB MIXED DRIED FRUIT
- 100 G/4 OZ FLAKED ALMONDS
- 100 G/4 OZ DARK MUSCOVADO OR MOLASSES SUGAR
- 1 EGG, SIZE 3, BEATEN
- 150 ML/¼ PINT WHISKY OR BRANDY
- 3 TBSP MILK
- BEATEN EGG, TO GLAZE

1 Set the oven to 180°C/350°F/Gas 4. Grease and base-line a 20cm/8inch loose-based or spring-clip round cake tin.

2 Divide the pastry into two pieces, two-thirds and one-third. Roll out the larger piece thinly into a round about 35cm/14inches in diameter. Use to line the cake tin, gently pressing it on to the bottom and sides of the tin, trying not to pleat it as this will spoil the appearance of the outside of the cake. Leave the pastry hanging over the sides of the tin. Cover with a tea towel and set aside.

3 Sift the flour, spices, cream of tartar and soda into a bowl. Mix in the dried fruit, almonds and sugar. Add the egg, whisky or brandy and milk and stir until combined and moist. Pack into the pastry case and smooth level. Fold the overhanging pastry edges over the filling.

4 Roll out the remaining pastry to a round to fit the top of the tin. Moisten the pastry edges in the tin, place the round on top and press together. Pinch the edges together in a fluted pattern to seal. Make six or seven large holes in the pastry lid with a skewer, then prick over the top with a fork, making an even pattern. Brush liberally with beaten egg.

5 Bake in the centre of the oven for about 2½ hours or until a warmed metal skewer inserted in the middle comes out clean. If the top begins to brown too quickly, cover with a sheet of brown paper or a sheet of greaseproof paper and several sheets of newspaper.

6 Leave to cool in the tin, then store for 4 weeks to allow the filling to mellow.

TO FREEZE: *Freezing speeds up the mellowing process of the filling, as it does for all fruit cakes. Store in a rigid container. Keeps for up to 4 months.*

Illustrated opposite page 144

$\mathcal{S}$IMNEL CAKE

*Traditionally, Simnel cake was made for Mothering Sunday. Girls
working in service were allowed to use up the leftover dried fruits
from the Christmas celebrations to make this cake as a present for
their mothers. Live-in servants quite often did not see their parents
for long periods of time, and these cakes, decorated with bunches of
wild spring flowers, must have been a very welcome gift. Nowadays,
Simnel cakes are often made for Easter, decorated with eleven balls
of almond paste to represent all of the apostles except for Judas.*

225 G/8 OZ PLAIN FLOUR

1 TSP BAKING POWDER

2 TSP MIXED SPICE

PINCH SALT

175 G/6 OZ BUTTER,
AT ROOM TEMPERATURE

175 G/6 OZ SOFT BROWN SUGAR

3 EGGS, SIZE 2

100 G/4 OZ RAISINS

175 G/6 OZ CURRANTS

100 G/4 OZ SULTANAS

50 G/2 OZ CHOPPED CANDIED
MIXED PEEL

50 G/2 OZ GLACÉ CHERRIES,
RINSED, DRIED AND HALVED

2 TBSP MILK

FINELY GRATED ZEST
1 ORANGE AND ½ LEMON

450 G/1LB ALMOND PASTE
(SEE PAGE 160)

2 TBSP APRICOT GLAZE
(SEE PAGE 169)

$\mathcal{1}$ Set the oven to 160°C/325°F/Gas 3. Grease and line an 18cm/7inch round deep
cake tin.

$\mathcal{2}$ Sift together the flour, baking powder, spice and salt. Cream the butter and sugar
together until light and fluffy. Beat the eggs into the mixture one at a time, adding a
little flour with each addition. Add the fruits and peel to the remaining flour and toss
lightly to coat, then fold into the creamed mixture with the milk and grated zests. Stir
well together.

3 Roll out one-third of the almond paste to a round the same size as the cake tin. Spoon half the cake mixture into the tin, place the almond paste round on top and cover with the remainder of the cake mixture. Smooth level. Bake for about 2 hours or until the centre of the cake is firm. Leave to cool in the tin, then turn out on to a wire rack and remove the lining paper.

4 When the cake is cold, brush the top with the apricot glaze. Roll out just over half the remaining almond paste to a round to fit the top of the cake. Place on the cake. Mark a criss-cross pattern in the middle, then flute up the edges of the paste like pastry. Roll the rest of the almond paste into eleven balls. Dab each with apricot jam and stick to the top, arranging in a ring. Add sugar or fresh flowers, and tie a nice bright ribbon round the outside.

N O T E : *The 18cm/7inch tin makes a deep cake. If you wish to make a shallower one, use a 20cm/8inch tin, and bake about 15 minutes less.*

T O   F R E E Z E : *Wrap whole cake or pieces in foil. Keeps for 3 months.*

Illustrated opposite page 97

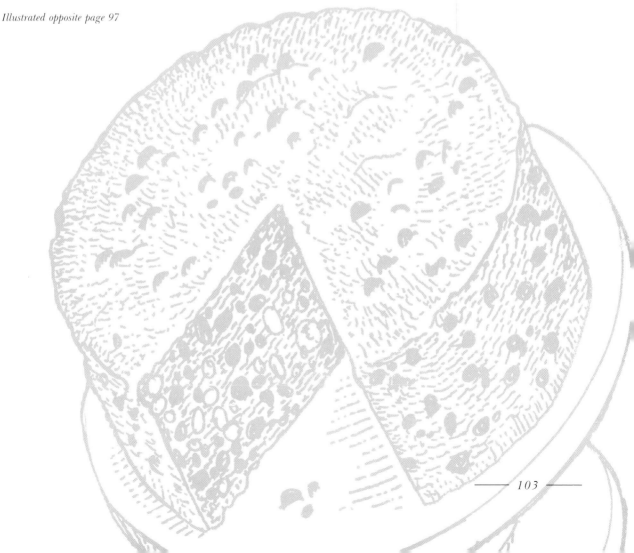

WHISKY FRUIT CAKE

*This is a really moist fruit cake made by the old-fashioned method
of simmering the fruit in liquid before mixing, which really plumps
it up. You can replace the whisky with dark rum, brandy or sherry,
but as mine is a Scottish household, we've usually the odd
'wee dram' around. This is a good cake for keeping in the cake tin
for 2–3 weeks.*

- 175 G/6 OZ STONED DATES, CHOPPED
- 175 G/6 OZ NO-NEED-TO-SOAK DRIED APRICOTS, CHOPPED
- 225 G/8 OZ RAISINS OR SULTANAS
- 100 G/4 OZ CHOPPED CANDIED MIXED PEEL
- 50 G/2 OZ GLACÉ CHERRIES, HALVED
- 150 G/5 OZ BUTTER
- 150 ML/¼ PINT MILK
- 5 TBSP GOLDEN SYRUP
- 3 TBSP WHISKY
- 225 G/8 OZ PLAIN WHOLEMEAL FLOUR
- 1 TSP MIXED SPICE
- 2 EGGS, SIZE 3
- ½ TSP BICARBONATE OF SODA
- DEMERARA SUGAR, TO DECORATE

1 Set the oven to 150°C/300°F/Gas 2. Grease and line a 20cm/8inch round deep cake tin.

2 Place the dried fruits, peel and cherries in a heavy-based saucepan with the butter, milk and syrup and heat gently until the butter has melted. Simmer for about 5 minutes, stirring regularly, then pour the mixture into a bowl. Leave it to cool for 30 minutes (this is important as the cake will not rise if the mixture is still warm when the soda is added). Stir in the whisky as the mixture cools.

3 Sift the flour and mixed spice together, then add any bran remaining in the sieve. When the fruit mixture is cold, beat in the eggs and soda, then stir in the flour. Spoon into the tin and make a small hollow in the centre.

4 Bake in the centre of the oven for about 1¾ hours or until the cake is firm to the touch in the centre. Sprinkle with demerara sugar whilst still hot, then leave to cool in the tin. Remove the lining paper and store in an airtight tin until needed.

TO FREEZE: *Wrap tightly in foil. Keeps for up to 6 months.*

$\mathcal{V}$INEGAR CAKE

This is an eggless cake that I make for a friend who has an allergy to eggs. You can't taste the vinegar, but it does give the cake a lovely tartness, which combines beautifully with a slice of cheese.

- 225 G/8 OZ BUTTER
- 450 G/1LB PLAIN FLOUR
- 450 G/1LB MIXED DRIED FRUIT
- 225 G/8 OZ DARK MUSCOVADO SUGAR

- 1 TSP BICARBONATE OF SODA
- 300 ML/½ PINT MILK
- 3 TBSP CIDER OR MALT VINEGAR

1 Set the oven to 200°C/400°F/Gas 6. Grease and line a 20cm/8inch square or 23cm/9inch round deep cake tin.

2 Rub the butter into the flour until the mixture resembles fine crumbs, then stir in the fruit and sugar. Sprinkle the bicarbonate of soda over the milk, then add the vinegar, which will make the mixture foam and froth. Add to the dry mix in the bowl and stir quickly together.

3 Spoon into the prepared tin and level the top. Bake for 20 minutes, then reduce the heat to 170°C/325°F/Gas 3 and continue baking for about 1½ hours or until firm to the touch. If the top starts to become too brown, cover with screwed-up dampened greaseproof paper. Leave to cool in the tin.

TO FREEZE: *Wrap in foil. Keeps for 3 months.*

*Tie brown paper around tin
to protect sides of cake*

*A skewer will come out clean
when cake is cooked*

ℬUTTERSCOTCH
FRUIT CAKE

*This is my favourite light fruit cake, which makes an excellent base
for all sorts of celebration cakes. It keeps well for about 4 weeks,
and has a delicious butterscotchy flavour.*

- 1 TBSP BLACK TREACLE
- 225 G/8 OZ BUTTER,
  AT ROOM TEMPERATURE
- 225 G/8 OZ SOFT LIGHT
  BROWN SUGAR
- ½ TSP ALMOND ESSENCE
- ½ TSP VANILLA ESSENCE
- 2 TBSP ORANGE MARMALADE

- 4 EGGS, SIZE 3, SEPARATED
- 275 G/10 OZ PLAIN FLOUR
- ½ TSP GROUND NUTMEG
- 400 G/14 OZ DRIED
  MIXED FRUIT
- 4 TBSP DARK RUM
- TOPPING (OPTIONAL,
  SEE STEP 5)

1 Set the oven to 170°C/325°F/Gas 3. Grease and line a 20cm/8inch square or
23cm/9inch round deep cake tin.

2 Cream together the treacle, butter and sugar until light and fluffy, then beat in
the essences and marmalade. Gradually add the egg yolks, beating well. Sift in the
flour and nutmeg, then sprinkle over the fruit and stir into the mixture.

3 Whisk the egg whites until they form soft peaks. Gently fold a little egg white into
the mixture to loosen it, then fold in the remainder, with 3 tbsp rum.

4 Spoon into the tin and smooth level. Bake in the centre of the oven for about 2½
hours or until a skewer inserted in the centre comes out clean. Leave to cool in the tin
for 15 minutes, then turn out on to a wire rack to cool completely. Peel away the
lining paper.

5 Sprinkle with 1 tbsp rum, or more if you are feeling generous, and store in an
airtight tin for 1 week. Eat plain, or decorate with almond paste (see page 160) and
royal or fondant icing (see page 162 or 164).

TO FREEZE: *Wrap in foil. Keeps for 2–3 months.*

SULTANA AND LEMON LOAVES

I make these easy teabreads for slicing and buttering at bazaars and fêtes. You can make them in batches of two and freeze or store them in airtight tins for up to 2 weeks. This is a great standby when your friends volunteer you to 'do the teas'.

- 450 G/1 LB SULTANAS
- 225 G/8 OZ DEMERARA SUGAR
- 300 ML/½ PINT WARM TEA, STRAINED
- 1 EGG, SIZE 3

- 2 TBSP LEMON OR LIME MARMALADE
- 225 G/8 OZ PLAIN FLOUR
- 225 G/8 OZ PLAIN WHOLEMEAL FLOUR
- 4 TSP BAKING POWDER

1 Place the sultanas, sugar and tea in a bowl and leave to soak overnight.

2 Set the oven to 170°C/325°F/Gas 3. Grease and base-line two 450g/1lb loaf tins.

3 Beat the egg and marmalade into the sultanas and liquid. Sift in the flours and baking powder, adding any bran left in the sieve. Mix together well. If dry, add 1–2 tbsp milk. Divide between the two tins and spread the tops level.

4 Bake in the centre of the oven for about 1½ hours or until the cakes are firm to the touch in the centre. Cool in the tins for 5 minutes, then turn out on to wire racks to cool completely. Serve sliced and buttered.

VARIATIONS: *Replace the sultanas with mixed dried fruit or raisins and the lemon marmalade with orange marmalade. For a malt loaf, replace the marmalade with malt extract.*

TO FREEZE: *Wrap in foil and pack in freezer bags. Keeps for up to 4 months.*

Illustrated opposite page 96

GEORGE WASHINGTON CAKE

The recipe for this cake was taken over to the USA from England in the eighteenth century.

- 350 G/12 OZ UNSALTED BUTTER OR BLOCK MARGARINE, AT ROOM TEMPERATURE
- 350 G/12 OZ CASTER SUGAR
- 4 EGGS, SIZE 3, SEPARATED
- 450 G/1 LB PLAIN FLOUR
- 1 TBSP BAKING POWDER
- 1 TSP GROUND MACE
- 1 TSP GROUND CINNAMON

- ½ TSP SALT
- 300 ML/½ PINT MILK
- 100 G/4 OZ RAISINS
- 50 G/2 OZ CURRANTS
- FINELY GRATED ZEST 1 LARGE LEMON
- FILLING AND TOPPING (SEE STEP 5)

1 Set the oven to 170°C/325°F/Gas 3. Grease and double-line a 23cm/9inch round or 20cm/8inch square deep cake tin.

2 Cream the fat and sugar together until light and fluffy, then beat in the egg yolks, adding a teaspoon of flour to help the mixture combine.

3 Sift the remaining flour, the baking powder, spices and salt together and fold alternately into the creamed mixture with the milk. Stir in the dried fruit and zest. Whisk the egg whites until they form soft peaks and fold in as lightly as possible.

4 Spoon into the tin. Bake for about 1½ hours or until a warmed skewer inserted in the centre comes out cleanly. Leave to cool in the tin for 10 minutes, then turn out on to a wire rack to cool completely.

5 Cut the cake in half horizontally and sandwich together with simple buttercream (see page 170). Spread the top with thin glacé icing (see page 166) or royal icing (see page 162) and let it dribble down the sides unevenly.

TO FREEZE: *Wrap in non-stick silicone paper, then foil. Keeps for 3 months.*

$\mathcal{W}$HAT WENT WRONG?

☞ THE FRUIT SINKS:

Dried fruits are heavy and if the mixture is too wet, the weighty fruits will drop to the bottom, so keep the mixture stiff enough to support the fruit. Rinse off any syrup from glacé cherries, dry them well and toss in flour, as syrupy cherries will sink. Wet fruit will also sink, so if you wash or soak it before use, pat it dry with a tea towel or kitchen paper before adding to the mixture.

☞ A HARD CRUST FORMS:

A crust will form if the oven is too hot, or if the cake is baked for too long or too near the top of the oven. A fruit cake baked for several hours must be protected by several layers of brown paper or newspaper wrapped around the tin to prevent a crust from forming.

☞ THE TOP SINKS IN THE MIDDLE:

Too much raising agent can cause this, as can overbeating after adding the eggs. Use of too small a tin, too cool an oven, underbaking, or slamming the door during baking can also cause this to happen.

☞ THE TOP CRACKS OR PEAKS:

This can be caused by too hot an oven, too dry a mixture, or using a shelf too near the top of the oven.

☞ THE CAKE SLOPES TO ONE SIDE:

This can be caused by not thoroughly preheating the oven, not positioning the cake centrally, or the shelf or oven itself not being level.

☞ THE COOKED CAKE HAS MOULD AFTER STORAGE:

Patches of mould can occur if the cake is stored in humid, wet, warm or steamy conditions, and usually occurs on an undercooked cake. Plastic storage boxes encourage mould, and should never be used to store fruit cakes for long periods, as they keep in moisture. Always use airtight tins or layers of foil for storage.

$\mathcal{N}$ UTTY CAKES

CHAPTER SIX

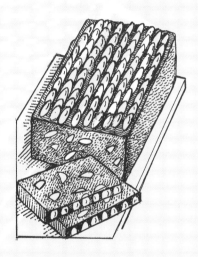

akes baked with nuts are truly delicious, moist and tender. Continental cakes and gâteaux are absolutely loaded with nuts of every description, and really make the most of these delectable morsels. Ground nuts impart a moist texture, and as they have a high fat content, they also enrich a cake.

When buying nuts, choose shops that have a rapid turnover of stock. Since nuts have such a high fat content, they can go rancid very quickly, which gives them an awful, bitter flavour. Do not buy nuts in bulk, as they do not have a long shelf life at home; only buy them when you need them. If you do have some left to store, keep them in a jar in a cool place for up to 4 months. Whole or shelled nuts can be frozen in polythene bags, but do label them clearly with the date, and don't keep them for longer than 12 months, or 3 months if toasted.

RIGHT (from top to bottom): Hazelnut Meringue Torte with Raspberry Cream Filling (see page 115); Frosted English Walnut Layer (see page 121); Almond, Grand Marnier and Strawberry Gâteau (see page 124).

LEFT (from top to bottom): Coffee and Walnut Gâteau (see page 117); Nutty Orange Kugelhupf (see page 122); Crunchy Topped Coconut Cake with Apricots (see page 120).

*Pour boiling water over
almonds to blanch*

*Remove nuts after a
few minutes*

Slip the nuts out of their skins

$\mathscr{U}$SING NUTS FOR BAKING

ALMONDS

Almonds can be bought blanched, flaked, slivered, chopped or ground, or you can buy the whole almonds and prepare them at home for real freshness.

Shelled almonds still have their skins on. To remove these, blanch the nuts in boiling water for a few minutes; the nuts will then slip easily out of the skins. It is easier to chop, split or grind blanched nuts while they are still warm.

To grind almonds, place them in a food processor and work until fine. Take care not to over-process as the natural oils from the nuts will be released, and they will be difficult to handle. Chop or process in small batches to make the job easier.

BRAZIL NUTS

These rich nuts have a wonderful flavour, and are more often sold in the shell. To crack them easily, place in the freezer for a few hours (this is particularly helpful if you have lots to shell). Brazils can be used whole or chopped, or you can slice them lengthways with a knife or peeler and toast them. Use as an outer coating for a gâteau instead of flaked almonds.

HAZELNUTS

Hazelnuts are sold whole, shelled in their skins, chopped or ground. Most cake recipes used toasted hazelnuts because toasting brings out their flavour. To toast, spread whole nuts on a baking sheet and place under a hot grill for a few minutes, shaking the sheet occasionally. To remove the feathery skins, rub the hot nuts in a tea towel and the skins will flake away. To grind the nuts, work them in a food processor in small amounts, taking care not to over-process as this makes them oily.

PISTACHIO NUTS

These sweet aromatic little nuts have a dark brown skin, but a wonderful bright green kernel, which makes them ideal for decoration. To remove the outer skins, blanch the nuts in boiling water for 1 minute, then slip them out of their skins while still warm. Use them whole or chopped.

WALNUTS

Walnuts are very oily and will turn rancid quickly, so should not be stored in bulk. Whole nuts will wither inside the shell if not eaten quickly. The larger the nuts, the more expensive and better quality they are. They can be bought in halves or pieces, and these are ideal for chopping or grinding. Chop them quickly in a food processor to prevent them releasing too much oil, or snip a small amount with kitchen scissors.

HAZELNUT MERINGUE TORTE WITH RASPBERRY CREAM FILLING

The meringue bases can be made well ahead of time and stored for 1–2 days before spreading with chocolate and sandwiching together with cream and raspberries.

- 150 G/5 OZ CHOPPED, TOASTED HAZELNUTS
- 5 EGG WHITES, SIZE 3
- 275 G/10 OZ CASTER SUGAR, STORED WITH A VANILLA POD
- 1 TSP LEMON JUICE

- 225 G/8 OZ PLAIN CHOCOLATE
- **FILLING:**
- 300 ML/½ PINT DOUBLE OR WHIPPING CREAM
- 225 G/8 OZ RASPBERRIES

1 Set the oven to 190°C/375°F/Gas 5. Grease and line two 20cm/8inch sandwich tins.

2 Place the nuts in a food processor, grinder or blender and grind them finely. Whisk the egg whites until they form stiff peaks, then add half the sugar, a tablespoon at a time, whisking after each addition. Stir the nuts and remaining sugar together, then fold them gently into the egg whites with the lemon juice, using a metal spoon.

3 Divide the meringue evenly between the tins and spread level. Bake in the centre of the oven for about 35 minutes. Leave to cool completely in the tins, then loosen the sides with a knife, turn out and peel away the lining paper.

4 Break the chocolate into pieces and melt gently in a heatproof bowl set over a pan of warm water, or in the microwave oven. Paint the underside of each meringue layer with a thin coat of chocolate, then leave to dry and set.

5 To make the filling, whip the cream until stiff, then fold in the raspberries. Place one meringue layer on a plate, chocolate side up, then spread with the cream and place the other meringue layer on top, chocolate side down. If liked, dredge with sifted icing sugar and decorate with any leftover raspberries. If you have a little melted chocolate left, place it in a paper piping bag (see page 182), cut a small hole in the tip and drizzle thin lines of chocolate across the top of the torte. Chill for 30 minutes before serving, to firm the cream.

Not suitable for freezing.

Illustrated opposite page 112

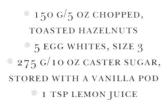

GÂTEAU SANS RIVAL

*This cake contains no flour, but lots of almonds. It makes a very
special party cake.*

- 100 G/4 OZ GROUND ALMONDS
- 150 G/5 OZ CASTER SUGAR
- 4 EGG WHITES, SIZE 3
- DOUBLE QUANTITY PRALINE
  (SEE PAGE 171), FINELY CRUSHED
- **FILLING:**
- 4 EGG YOLKS, SIZE 3
- 200 ML/7 FL OZ WHIPPING
  CREAM, WHIPPED

- 75 G/3 OZ CASTER SUGAR
- 50 G/2 OZ BUTTER
- **DECORATION:**
- 225 G/8 OZ ALMOND PASTE
  (SEE PAGE 160)
- 50 G/2 OZ FLAKED ALMONDS,
  LIGHTLY TOASTED

1 Set the oven to 200°C/400°F/Gas 6. Line three baking sheets with non-stick
silicone paper, and mark a 20cm/8inch square on each.

2 Mix the ground almonds with the sugar. Whisk the egg whites until stiff, then
gradually fold in the almond mixture, keeping the mixture as light as possible. Divide
the mixture between the three baking sheets, spreading it inside the squares, and
level with a palette knife. Bake for 12–15 minutes or until firm.

3 Leave the meringue layers to cool on the baking sheets until firm enough to
handle, then peel away the paper.

4 To make the filling, place all the ingredients in a saucepan and cook gently,
stirring, until the mixture thickens. Do not allow to boil at any time. Pour into a bowl
to cool. When cold, add the crushed praline.

5 Sandwich the meringue layers together with praline cream, then trim any edges
straight with a sharp knife. Spread the remaining filling thinly over the top and
round the sides of the gâteau.

6 Colour the almond paste if liked, then roll it out into a thin strip long enough to
go round the sides of the cake and wide enough to cover the layers. Press into place.
Re-roll the trimmings and cut into flowers or other shapes such as hearts.

7 Sprinkle the top of the gâteau with the flaked almonds, then decorate with the
almond paste shapes.

Not suitable for freezing.

COFFEE AND WALNUT GÂTEAU

This cake makes an ideal large birthday or celebration cake, and can be covered in fondant icing (see page 164) and decorated to suit the occasion.

- 350 G/12 OZ UNSALTED BUTTER, AT ROOM TEMPERATURE
- 350 G/12 OZ SOFT LIGHT BROWN SUGAR
- 6 EGGS, SIZE 3, BEATEN
- 350 G/12 OZ SELF-RAISING FLOUR
- 1 TSP BAKING POWDER
- 1 TBSP INSTANT COFFEE GRANULES
- 100 G/4 OZ SHELLED WALNUTS, CHOPPED

- **TOPPING:**
- CRÈME AU BEURRE (SEE PAGE 167), MADE WITH 225 G/8 OZ CASTER SUGAR, 4 EGG YOLKS, SIZE 3, AND 275 G/10 OZ UNSALTED BUTTER
- **DECORATION:**
- 100 G/4 OZ WALNUT HALVES
- 4 TBSP MAPLE SYRUP

1 Set the oven to 180°C/350°F/Gas 4. Grease and base-line a round 23cm/9inch loose-based or spring-clip cake tin.

2 Cream the butter and sugar together until light and fluffy, then gradually beat in the eggs, adding a little of the self-raising flour with each addition to prevent the mixture from curdling.

3 Sift the remaining flour and baking powder together and fold into the creamed mixture. Dissolve the coffee in 2 tbsp boiling water and cool slightly, then add to the mixture with the walnuts.

4 Spoon the mixture into the tin. Bake in the centre of the oven for 1 hour 10 minutes or until well risen and firm to the touch in the centre. Leave to cool in the tin for 5 minutes, then turn out on to a wire rack and peel away the lining paper. Cool completely.

5 Cut the cake in half horizontally, then sandwich the layers together with one-quarter of the crème au beurre. Spread the remainder over the top and sides of the cake and smooth with a palette knife. Decorate the top with the walnut halves, placed in rings, then drizzle the maple syrup over, letting it trickle down the sides.

TO FREEZE: *Open-freeze filled and iced cake, without the nuts and syrup, in a rigid container. Keeps for 2 months.*

Illustrated opposite page 113

ℬANANA AND NUT TEABREAD

This is a really quick bake and a perfect way of using up those mushy old bananas left in the fruit bowl.

- 200 G/7 OZ SELF-RAISING FLOUR
- PINCH SALT
- ¼ TSP BICARBONATE OF SODA
- 75 G/3 OZ SOFT TUB MARGARINE
- 100 G/4 OZ SOFT LIGHT BROWN SUGAR
- 1 EGG, SIZE 2, BEATEN
- 100 G/4 OZ RAISINS OR CHOPPED DATES
- 75 G/3 OZ SHELLED WALNUTS, CHOPPED
- 2 LARGE VERY RIPE BANANAS, WELL MASHED
- 1–2 TBSP GOLDEN SYRUP

1 Set the oven to 180°C/350°F/Gas 4. Grease and line a 450g/1lb loaf tin.

2 Sift the flour, salt and soda into a bowl. Add all the other ingredients, except the golden syrup, and beat well together. Add 1–2 tbsp milk if the mixture is too dry.

3 Spoon into the prepared tin. Bake in the centre of the oven for about 1 hour or until firm in the middle and just shrinking away from the tin. Leave to cool in the tin for 10 minutes, then turn out on to a wire rack.

4 Brush the top of the loaf with the golden syrup while still warm, to give a sticky glaze. Serve warm or cold, sliced and buttered.

VARIATION: *Omit the walnuts and add 50g/2oz rinsed, chopped glacé cherries.*

TO FREEZE: *Wrap whole loaf or slices in a freezer bag. Keeps for 3 months.*

ℳOIST ALMOND GÂTEAU

The ground almonds and spirit in this cake make it beautifully moist. It can be baked a few days ahead, and decorated with caramel-dipped almonds or fondant icing for a special occasion.

- 100 G/4 OZ UNSALTED BUTTER, AT ROOM TEMPERATURE
- 100 G/4 OZ CASTER SUGAR
- 2 EGGS, SIZE 3, BEATEN
- 100 G/4 OZ SELF-RAISING FLOUR
- 75 G/3 OZ GROUND ALMONDS
- 2–3 TBSP KIRSCH, MARSALA OR WATER
- TOPPING (SEE STEP 4)

1 Set the oven to 180°C/350°F/Gas 4. Grease and line a 20cm/8inch round deep cake tin or a 450g/1lb loaf tin.

2 Cream the butter and sugar together until pale and fluffy, then gradually beat in the eggs, adding a little flour with each addition. Stir the almonds and remaining flour together, then gradually fold into the creamed mixture with the Kirsch, Marsala or water, to give a soft consistency.

3 Spoon into the tin and spread level. If using the loaf tin, make a hollow in the middle. Bake the round cake for about 50 minutes or until firm, or the loaf for 1–1¼ hours. Leave to cool in the tin, then store in an airtight tin.

4 Decorate with caramel-dipped almonds (see page 171), arranged into flowers, or with fondant icing (see page 164).

TO FREEZE: *Wrap undecorated cake in foil. Keeps for 2 months.*

ℋALVA CAKE FOR EASTER

This cake is made in Cyprus for the Easter celebrations. It is very moist and refreshing and keeps well. It is ideal for an informal Easter buffet party.

- 175 G/6 OZ BUTTER, AT ROOM TEMPERATURE
- 175 G/6 OZ CASTER SUGAR
- 4 EGGS, SIZE 3
- 175 G/6 OZ SEMOLINA
- 1 TSP GROUND CINNAMON
- 50 G/2 OZ GROUND ALMONDS
- 50 G/2 OZ FLAKED ALMONDS
- **SYRUP:**
- 225 G/8 OZ CASTER SUGAR
- 600 ML/1 PINT WATER
- 1 TBSP LEMON JUICE
- 1 CINNAMON STICK

1 Set the oven to 190°C/375°F/Gas 5. Grease and line an 18cm/7inch round deep cake tin.

2 Cream the butter and sugar together until light and fluffy. Beat in the eggs one at a time, then beat in the semolina and cinnamon. Fold in the ground almonds and half the flaked almonds, reserving the rest for the top.

3 Turn the mixture into the tin. Bake for 40 minutes or until a skewer inserted in the middle comes out clean.

4 Make the syrup while the cake is baking: place all the ingredients in a large pan and heat gently until every grain of sugar has dissolved. Boil rapidly for 15 minutes until a syrup is formed, then remove the cinnamon stick.

5 Pour the syrup over the warm cake in the tin and leave to cool completely, in the tin. When cold, sprinkle over the remaining almonds.

TO FREEZE: *Wrap cake in foil and seal. Keeps for 2 months.*

CRUNCHY TOPPED
COCONUT CAKE
WITH APRICOTS

*This crunchy topped coconut cake is delicious served just warm with
cream or yogurt, or cold on its own.*

CRUNCHY TOPPING:
- 25 G/1 OZ BUTTER OR BLOCK MARGARINE
- 40 G/1½ OZ PLAIN FLOUR
- 50 G/2 OZ DEMERARA SUGAR
- 25 G/1 OZ DESICCATED COCONUT

CAKE:
- 175 G/6 OZ BUTTER OR BLOCK MARGARINE, AT ROOM TEMPERATURE
- 175 G/6 OZ CASTER SUGAR
- 3 EGGS, SIZE 3, BEATEN
- 175 G/6 OZ SELF-RAISING FLOUR
- 6 FRESH APRICOTS, PEELED, STONED AND CHOPPED OR 1 × 225 G/8 OZ TIN APRICOTS, DRAINED AND CHOPPED
- 75 G/3 OZ DESICCATED COCONUT

1 Set the oven to 160°C/325°F/Gas 3. Grease and base-line a 20cm/8inch round loose-based or spring-clip cake tin.

2 Make the topping by rubbing the fat into the flour until it resembles fine crumbs, then stirring in the remaining ingredients.

3 To make the cake, cream the fat with the sugar until light and fluffy. Beat in the eggs gradually, adding a little flour with each addition to prevent curdling. Fold in the remaining flour, the apricots and coconut.

4 Turn the mixture into the prepared tin and smooth the top level. Sprinkle the topping in an even layer over the cake mixture. Bake in the centre of the oven for about 1¼ hours or until the middle of the cake is firm. Leave to cool in the tin for 10 minutes, then remove the sides of the tin and cool the cake completely on a wire rack.

Not suitable for freezing.

Illustrated opposite page 113

FROSTED ENGLISH WALNUT LAYER

I still remember being taken out to tea at the local Fuller's Tea Shop as a child. The pièce de résistance was their famous frosted walnut cake. They were so irresistible we usually bought one to take home in a box. This obviously accounts for a life-long addiction to cakes!

- 225 G/8 OZ SELF-RAISING FLOUR
- 1 TSP BAKING POWDER
- 225 G/8 OZ BUTTER OR BLOCK MARGARINE, AT ROOM TEMPERATURE
- 225 G/8 OZ SOFT LIGHT BROWN SUGAR
- 4 EGGS, SIZE 2, BEATEN

- 75 G/3 OZ SHELLED WALNUTS, FINELY CHOPPED
- 1 TBSP BLACK TREACLE
- 1 QUANTITY SEVEN-MINUTE FROSTING (SEE PAGE 166)
- 8 WALNUT HALVES, TO DECORATE

1 Grease and base-line three 20cm/8inch sandwich tins. Set the oven to 170°C/325°F/Gas 3.

2 Sift the flour and baking powder together. Cream the fat and sugar together until light and fluffy, then beat in the eggs gradually, adding a little flour with each addition. Fold in the remaining flour with the chopped walnuts and black treacle.

3 Divide the mixture among the three tins and level the tops. Bake as centrally in the oven as possible for about 30 minutes or until springy to the touch in the centre. Leave to cool in the tins for 5 minutes, then turn out on to wire racks and cool completely.

4 Sandwich the cakes together thinly with frosting, then cover the top and sides, flicking and swirling the frosting with a palette knife. Decorate with the walnut halves in a ring, and leave on the serving place to allow the frosting to set.

TO FREEZE: *Wrap unfilled layers in freezer bags. Keeps for 3 months.*

Illustrated opposite page 112

Nutty Orange
KUGELHUPF

The kugelhupf or gugelhupf mould is round and deep with fluted or patterned sides and a chimney in the middle. The mould comes from Southern Germany and Austria, and bakes wonderful cakes because the heat is distributed so evenly in the centre. Traditionally, yeasted mixtures were baked in these moulds, but light sponge and fruit cakes work just as well.

- 225 G/8 OZ BUTTER OR BLOCK MARGARINE, AT ROOM TEMPERATURE
- 225 G/8 OZ SOFT LIGHT BROWN SUGAR
- 3 EGGS, SIZE 3
- 225 G/8 OZ SELF-RAISING FLOUR
- FINELY GRATED ZEST 1 ORANGE
- 50 G/2 OZ CHOPPED CANDIED MIXED PEEL
- 50 G/2 OZ CHOPPED MIXED NUTS
- **SYRUP:**
- 3 TBSP CLEAR HONEY
- 4 TBSP FRESH ORANGE JUICE
- **DECORATION:**
- 100 G/4 OZ ICING SUGAR
- 1 TBSP ORANGE JUICE
- 2 TBSP CHOPPED MIXED NUTS

1 Brush a 1.75 litre/3 pint kugelhupf mould with melted lard. Set the oven to 190°C/375°F/Gas 5.

2 Cream the fat and sugar together until light and fluffy, then beat in the eggs, one at a time, adding a little flour with each to prevent curdling. Fold in the remaining flour, the zest, peel and nuts, with 1 tbsp of cold water.

3 Spoon into the prepared mould and smooth the top level. Bake in the centre of the oven for about 1 hour or until firm to the touch and golden. Leave to cool in the mould for 2 minutes, then turn out on to a wire rack to cool completely.

4 When cold, place the honey and orange juice in a saucepan or microwave bowl and heat gently to melt the honey. Brush over the cake, and leave to cool.

5 To decorate, sift the icing sugar into a bowl and stir in the orange juice until well blended. Drizzle this glacé icing over the top and down the sides of the cake, then sprinkle the chopped nuts in a ring round the top. Alternatively, just dust the kugelhupf with sifted icing sugar to give a pretty snow-capped effect.

TO FREEZE: *Wrap undecorated cake in foil. Keeps for 2 months.*

Illustrated opposite page 113

ITALIAN FRUIT AND NUT FESTIVE RING

This cake contains very little flour, and the fruit and nuts are almost stuck to each other. It is a lovely cake to have in the tin around Christmas time, and looks very pretty with its glazed fruit top.

- 225 G/8 OZ STONED DATES
- 225 G/8 OZ SHELLED BRAZIL NUTS
- 100 G/4 OZ GLACÉ CHERRIES
- 50 G/2 OZ DARK MUSCOVADO SUGAR
- 50 G/2 OZ PLAIN FLOUR
- ½ TSP MIXED SPICE
- ¼ TSP BAKING POWDER
- 50 G/2 OZ CHOPPED CANDIED MIXED PEEL
- 2 TBSP DARK RUM OR SHERRY
- 1 EGG, SIZE 2, BEATEN
- ½ TSP VANILLA ESSENCE
- TOPPING (SEE STEP 4)

1 Grease and line an 18cm/7inch ring mould or a 450g/1lb loaf tin. Set the oven to 150°C/300°F/Gas 2.

2 Chop the dates, nuts and cherries roughly into large pieces and put in a bowl. Add the sugar, and sift in the flour, spice and baking powder. Stir to mix. Place the peel and rum or sherry in a small pan and heat gently to soften the peel. Cool slightly, then add to the bowl with the egg and vanilla essence. Mix together well.

3 Spoon into the mould or tin and press down level. Bake for 1¼–1½ hours, covering with foil if the cake starts to overbrown. Cool in the tin for 5 minutes, then turn out on to a wire rack to cool completely.

4 When cold, brush with apricot glaze (see page 169) or honey, and decorate with candied peel, fruit and nuts, plus a red ribbon bow.

TO FREEZE: *Wrap undecorated cake in foil. Keeps for 6 months.*

Almond, Grand Marnier and Strawberry Gâteau

This larger cake makes a good centrepiece for a family christening or party. You can easily make the cake base ahead of time, then decorate with lots of luscious strawberries just before serving.

- 175 G/6 OZ BUTTER, AT ROOM TEMPERATURE
- 175 G/6 OZ CASTER SUGAR
- FINELY GRATED ZEST 1 ORANGE
- 3 EGGS, SIZE 2, BEATEN
- 175 G/6 OZ SELF-RAISING FLOUR
- 2 TBSP ORANGE JUICE
- 50 G/2 OZ GROUND ALMONDS

FILLING AND DECORATION:
- 4 TBSP GRAND MARNIER OR OTHER ORANGE LIQUEUR
- 275 G/10 OZ FRESH STRAWBERRIES
- 300 ML/½ PINT DOUBLE CREAM, WHIPPED
- 100 G/4 OZ FLAKED ALMONDS
- ICING SUGAR

1 Set the oven to 170°C/325°F/Gas 3. Grease and line a 20cm/8inch round deep cake tin.

2 Cream the butter, sugar and zest together until very light and fluffy. Beat in the eggs, a little at a time, adding a teaspoon of flour if necessary to prevent the mixture from curdling. Fold in the orange juice, then sift in the remaining flour with the ground almonds. Fold lightly together until a soft consistency is reached.

3 Spoon into the tin. Bake in the centre of the oven for about 1¼ hours or until the sides are slightly shrunken away from the tin and the top is springy. Cool in the tin for 3 minutes, then turn out on to a wire rack and peel away the lining paper. Leave to cool completely.

4 Cut the cold cake in half horizontally, and sprinkle each half with 1 tbsp Grand Marnier. Keep aside 10–12 strawberries for decoration; hull and slice the rest and place on a plate. Sprinkle over the remaining liqueur and leave to soak for 2 hours.

5 To assemble the cake, divide the cream in half. Fold the sliced strawberries and their liquid into one half, and spread this on to the bottom cake layer. Set the other layer on top. Place neatly on a plate, then spread the remaining cream over the top and sides of the cake, smoothing with a palette knife.

6 Press the flaked almonds on to the sides of the cake thickly to cover. Cut thick strips of greaseproof paper and place diagonally across the top of the cake. Sift icing sugar over the top, then remove the paper strips, leaving a diagonal pattern. Halve the reserved strawberries, leaving the green tops attached, and arrange on the cake in diagonal lines, between the icing sugar. Chill until ready to serve.

TO FREEZE: *Wrap unsplit, undecorated cake in foil. Keeps for 3 months.*

Illustrated opposite page 112

GRATED CHOCOLATE
AND HAZELNUT GÂTEAU

*This cake has a combination of flavours: when you first bite into it,
it tastes of hazelnuts, then the secondary flavour of grated chocolate
comes through. A wonderful experience!*

- 200 G/7 OZ UNSALTED BUTTER, AT ROOM TEMPERATURE
- 175 G/6 OZ SOFT LIGHT BROWN SUGAR
- 3 EGGS, SIZE 3, SEPARATED
- 75 G/3 OZ SELF-RAISING FLOUR
- 75 G/3 OZ SKINNED HAZELNUTS, FINELY GROUND
- 100 G/4 OZ PLAIN CHOCOLATE, FINELY GRATED
- PINCH SALT
- 1 TBSP BRANDY (OPTIONAL)
- **CHOCOLATE GANACHE:**
- 150 ML/¼ PINT DOUBLE CREAM
- 100 G/4 OZ PLAIN CHOCOLATE, BROKEN INTO PIECES

1 Set the oven to 170°C/325°F/Gas 3. Grease and line a 900g/2lb loaf tin.

2 Cream the butter and sugar together until light and fluffy. Beat in the egg yolks one by one, then gently fold in the flour. Stir in the ground hazelnuts and grated chocolate.

3 Whisk the egg whites with the salt until they form floppy peaks. Fold a little into the mixture to loosen it, then fold in the remaining egg white gently.

4 Turn into the tin. Bake in the centre of the oven for 1¼ hours, then cool in the tin for 5 minutes. Turn out on to a wire rack to cool and peel away the lining paper. Sprinkle over the brandy if used.

5 To make the ganache filling, put the cream in a small saucepan and bring to the boil. Remove from the heat, add the chocolate and stir until melted. Pour into a bowl and leave to cool for 30 minutes, then whisk the mixture for 4–5 minutes with an electric mixer until it becomes very pale and fluffy. Chill for 15 minutes.

6 Split the cake into three horizontally and sandwich the layers together with ganache. Pipe rosettes of ganache on top or dredge with sifted icing sugar and decorate with fresh fruit such as cherries and strawberries.

TO FREEZE: *Wrap unfilled cake in foil. Keeps for 6 months.*

Illustrated opposite page 128

MICROWAVE BAKING

CHAPTER SEVEN

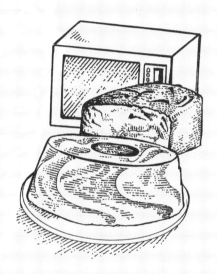

A new method of cooking — by microwave — has brought many advantages with it. Foods can be cooked in a matter of minutes, including many cakes. If you need to bake a cake in a hurry, then the microwave oven really does come into its own, although you do miss out on all those lovely aromas that normally fill the kitchen. When you have no space left in your conventional oven, then use the microwave for a quick bake — this is especially useful to help busy mothers survive children's party catering or comes to the rescue when those 'unexpected guests' turn up.

There are new and simple rules to be observed when using this source of power, so you will not be able to use your favourite baking recipes without adapting them first. The ones on the following pages have been specially created just for the microwave oven.

RIGHT (from top to bottom): Grated Chocolate and Hazelnut Gâteau (see page 125); Napoleons (see page 76); Angel Cake (see page 27), with Seven-minute Frosting (see page 166) and a raspberry coulis.

LEFT (from top to bottom): Cherry Cake (see page 133); Rich Fruit Ring Cake (see page 134); Sticky Gingercake (see page 132).

Shield corners with
foil squares

Test cake while surface
is still wet

A ring-shaped cake dish is best

ℬAKING MICROWAVE CAKES

Microwave-baked cakes rise well, but their texture and flavour are slightly different from cakes baked conventionally. As this is essentially a moist form of cooking, there is no dry heat to bake a brown crust on the outside; therefore, the cakes may be pale, and will need decorating. Here are a few points that need to be followed:

☞ When trying a new recipe, use a deeper container than you think necessary. Cakes can rise up very high, before falling back and setting. Also, only half fill dishes.

☞ Circular containers with rounded corners and straight sides are best for cakes. Pyrex soufflé dishes or casseroles can double up as cake tins. Avoid square containers with sharp corners, as the corners tend to over-cook. If you do use them, shield the corners with small pieces of foil.

☞ A ring-shaped cake dish is ideal for micro-bakes as the centres of most cakes are slower to cook, and this eliminates the problem. If you don't have a ring-shaped dish, stand an upturned microproof tumbler inside a large round dish.

☞ Lightly grease dishes and line them with non-stick silicone paper, but do not dredge with flour, as it will form a soggy crust on the cooked cake.

☞ Cakes look more appetizing if made with wholemeal flour, dark brown sugar, treacle or syrup to give colour.

☞ Cakes with a really high proportion of sugar will dry easily, so don't use these or meringue-type recipes. Make sure that all sugar is well rubbed or creamed in, as lumps of sugar will burn easily.

☞ To convert your favourite recipe for micro-baking you will need to add extra liquid in the form of water, milk, egg or fruit juice. Add about 1 tbsp liquid per egg for sponges and light cakes. Dried fruit in fruit cakes will dry up if not softened first. Microwave it in fruit juice or water for 3 minutes on High (100% power) to soften it first, then leave to cool and plump up. Add the liquid from the fruit and enough extra liquid to give a really soft dropping consistency to the mixture.

☞ Place the cake dish on an upturned soup plate, saucer or trivet. The microwaves need to reach the cake from all angles to cook it evenly.

☞ The top of a cake may look sticky and uncooked, but don't over-cook it. Putting it back in the oven will result in a dry cake which stales quickly.

☞ Do not turn cakes out immediately when cooked. They need 15 minutes standing time to continue to cook and settle down as they cool. Heavy mixtures like fruit cakes need a longer standing time.

☞ Turn cakes out on to a wire rack lined with non-stick silicone paper, otherwise as the cake dries and solidifies it will stick to the rack. If there are any uncooked spots on the cake, don't put it back into the container, but slide it into the oven on the paper and finish cooking in short bursts.

☞ Do not cover cakes with microwave-safe cling film, as you do in much microwave cooking. The steam needs to escape from cakes.

☞ Test the cake when the surface is still wet. Scratch the surface and lift with the point of a knife. Although the top is wet, the area underneath should be cooked. The cake will finish setting and drying as it cools.

☞ Cook sponge batters on High (100% power). The lower power settings pulsate and cause the cake to rise and fall repeatedly, which knocks out the air. Cook rich fruit cakes on Defrost (30% power) to give gentle slow cooking.

☞ Packet cake mixes cook well in the microwave. Add 2–3 extra tbsp liquid or as the packet instructs.

Gently ease cake off wire rack

*Turn cake on to
non-stick paper*

MOIST CHOCOLATE CAKE

- 100 G/4 OZ GOLDEN SYRUP
- 100 G/4 OZ DARK MUSCOVADO SUGAR
- 100 G/4 OZ SOFT TUB MARGARINE
- 175 G/6 OZ SELF-RAISING FLOUR

- 50 G/ 2 OZ COCOA POWDER
- 150 ML/¼ PINT MILK
- 1 EGG, SIZE 3, BEATEN
- 1 TSP FINELY GRATED ORANGE ZEST (OPTIONAL)
- 225 G/8 OZ PLAIN CHOCOLATE

1 Butter a 20cm/8inch microwave-proof ring mould. Place the syrup, sugar and margarine in a microwave-proof bowl and cook on High (100% power) for 2 minutes, to melt. Leave to cool for 10 minutes.

2 Sift the flour and cocoa powder into the bowl, then beat in the milk, egg and zest if used. Spoon into the mould and set on an upturned plate. Cook for 5 minutes on High (100% power), then leave to stand for 10 minutes before turning out.

3 When the cake is cold, break up the chocolate and melt it in a microwave-proof bowl in the microwave oven. Spread over the cake and leave to cool and set. Alternatively cover the cake with quick fudge icing (see opposite).

STICKY GINGERCAKE

- 75 G/3 OZ SOFT TUB MARGARINE
- 175 G/6 OZ BLACK TREACLE
- 50 G/2 OZ SOFT DARK BROWN SUGAR
- 2 TBSP GINGER PRESERVE
- 7 TBSP MILK
- ½ TSP BICARBONATE OF SODA

- 75 G/3 OZ SELF-RAISING FLOUR
- 75 G/3 OZ PLAIN FLOUR
- 2 TSP GROUND GINGER
- 1 EGG, SIZE 2, BEATEN
- DEMERARA SUGAR, TO DREDGE

1 Grease and base-line an 18cm/7inch round microwave-proof cake dish.

2 Place the margarine, treacle, sugar and ginger preserve in a microwave-proof bowl and cook on High (100% power) for 1 minute to melt. Warm the milk in a separate bowl on High (100% power) for 30 seconds, then stir in the bicarbonate of soda.

3 Sift the flours and ginger together into a bowl, add the melted mixture, milk and egg and beat together.

4 Spoon into the prepared dish and set on an upturned plate. Cook on High (100% power) for 8 minutes, turning the dish halfway through the cooking. Leave to stand for 5 minutes, then turn out. Dredge with demerara sugar and cool completely.

Illustrated opposite page 129

CHERRY CAKE

* 100 G/4 OZ BUTTER,
AT ROOM TEMPERATURE
* 225 G/8 OZ CASTER SUGAR
* 2 EGGS, SIZE 3, BEATEN
* 200 G/7 OZ SELF-RAISING FLOUR
* 25 G/1 OZ GROUND ALMONDS
* 5 TBSP EVAPORATED MILK

* 75 G/3 OZ GLACÉ CHERRIES,
RINSED, DRIED AND QUARTERED
* **DECORATION:**
* 100 G/4 OZ ICING SUGAR,
SIFTED
* GLACÉ CHERRIES

1 Grease and base-line an 18cm/7inch round cake dish or 900g/2lb microwave-proof loaf tin.

2 Cream the butter and sugar together until light and fluffy, then beat in the eggs gradually. Sift in the flour and almonds, then fold in with the milk and 5 tbsp water. Fold in the quartered cherries gently.

3 Spoon into the prepared dish and set on an upturned plate. Cook on High (100% power) for 8 minutes. Leave to stand for 10 minutes before turning out.

4 To make the icing, beat the sugar and 1 tbsp water together. Drizzle over the cold cake, letting it trickle down the sides. Decorate with glacé cherries.

Illustrated opposite page 129

QUICK FUDGE ICING

* 50 G/2 OZ BUTTER
* 200 G/7 OZ ICING SUGAR,
SIFTED

* 25 G/1 OZ COCOA POWDER,
SIFTED
* 1 TBSP MILK OR CREAM

1 Place all the ingredients plus 1 tbsp boiling water in a microwave-proof bowl and cook on High (100% power) for 10 seconds. Beat well and cook for a further 10–15 seconds. Beat quickly until really smooth. Cool, then beat or whisk again and spread evenly over the moist chocolate cake.

RICH FRUIT RING CAKE

- 150 G/6 OZ BUTTER, AT ROOM TEMPERATURE
- 150 G/6 OZ MOLASSES OR DARK MUSCOVADO SUGAR
- 4 EGGS, SIZE 3, BEATEN
- 2 TBSP BLACK TREACLE
- 2 TBSP DARK RUM
- 1 TBSP GRAVY BROWNING
- 100 G/4 OZ PLAIN WHOLEMEAL FLOUR
- 100 G/4 OZ SELF-RAISING FLOUR
- 1 TBSP MIXED SPICE
- 50 G/2 OZ FINELY GRATED CARROT
- 400 G/14 OZ MIXED DRIED FRUIT, PRE-SOAKED OR PLUMPED
- 100 G/4 OZ GLACÉ CHERRIES, RINSED, DRIED AND HALVED
- 50 G/2 OZ FLAKED ALMONDS OR CHOPPED WALNUTS
- 2 TBSP MILK

1 Grease a 2.5litre/4pint microwave-proof ring mould and dust with caster sugar.

2 Cream the butter and sugar together until light and fluffy, then gradually beat in the eggs, treacle, rum and gravy browning, adding a little flour with each addition to prevent curdling. Sift the remaining flours and spice into the mixture, add the bran from the sieve, then stir in with the carrot, dried fruit, cherries, nuts and milk.

3 Spoon the mixture into the greased ring mould and tap to remove any air pockets. Set the mould on an upturned plate and cook on Low or Defrost (30% power) for 35–40 minutes, turning the cake 2–3 times during cooking. The cake is done when a skewer inserted into the deepest part comes out clean. The surface may still appear sticky. Leave to stand for 25 minutes, then turn out on to a wire rack to cool completely. If liked, decorate with crystallized fruits. Store in an airtight tin for 1 week before cutting.

Illustrated opposite page 129

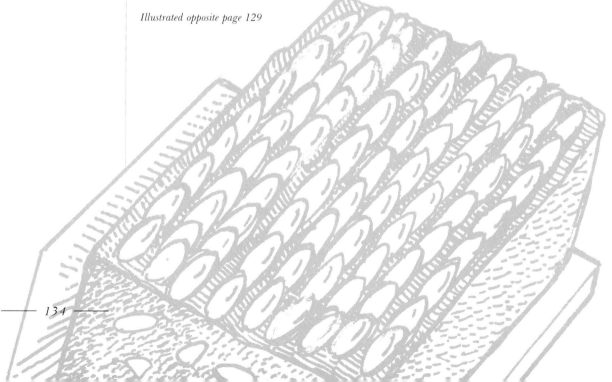

QUEEN CAKES

- 100 G/4 OZ SOFT TUB
  MARGARINE
- 100 G/4 OZ CASTER OR SOFT
  LIGHT BROWN SUGAR
- 2 EGGS, SIZE 3, BEATEN
- 100 G/4 OZ SELF-RAISING FLOUR

- 50 G/2 OZ CURRANTS
- ½ TSP FINELY GRATED
  LEMON ZEST
- 2–3 TBSP MILK
- TOPPING (SEE STEP 4)

1 Arrange six doubled paper cases in a microwave-proof bun tray.

2 Place all the ingredients in a large bowl and beat together until smooth and the mixture has a soft dropping consistency.

3 Half fill the paper cases. Cook, in batches, on High (100% power) for 1 minute or until risen but still slightly moist on the surface. Place on a wire rack to cool.

4 As the cakes are so pale, cover with glacé icing (see page 166) or quick fudge icing (see page 133).

VARIATIONS: *Omit the currants and replace with 50g/2oz of the following: sultanas, finely chopped dates, chocolate chips, chopped glacé cherries or angelica.*

BANANA AND
WALNUT CAKE

This is a quickly made moist cake that keeps well in a tin.

- 175 G/6 OZ SOFT DARK
  BROWN SUGAR
- 175 G/6 OZ SOFT TUB
  MARGARINE
- 3 EGGS

- 175 G/6 OZ WHOLEWHEAT
  SELF-RAISING FLOUR
- 2 MEDIUM BANANAS
- 60 ML/4 TBSP EVAPORATED MILK
- 100 G/4 OZ WALNUTS, CHOPPED

1 Grease and base line a 23cm(9in) round dish.

2 Put the sugar, margarine, eggs and flour into a bowl and mix lightly. Mash the bananas with the evaporated milk, and beat into the mixture with half the walnuts.

3 Pour into the dish and spread level. Cook on High for 4 minutes, then sprinkle over the remaining walnuts. Cook for a further 4–5 minutes or until the centre is cooked.

4 Leave to stand for 5 minutes before turning out, then slice when cold.

YEAST BAKING

CHAPTER EIGHT

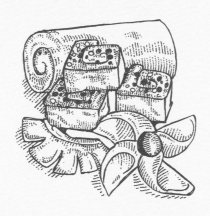

Baking with yeast is a true pleasure, and one of the most rewarding pastimes ever. Kneading a large piece of dough until it is smooth must also be one of the most natural ways of relaxing and relieving stress.

Enriched doughs go way back into history, and were the first type of risen cake. They are the most delicious of cakes, moist, rich and delectable. In many parts of the world they double up as breakfast, but you can really eat cakes at any time of day or night.

There is still something rather magical about watching dough rise, shaping it and then filling the house with that unmistakable aroma that only yeast bakes produce. It is well worth all the extra time and effort that is involved, so try a few of the following recipes, I'm sure you'll soon be hooked.

ℬAKING WITH YEAST

Knead yeast dough well until
smooth and elastic

☞ Fresh yeast is preferable to dried, if you can find it. It can be difficult to obtain – try bakers or health food shops, or buy some in bulk and freeze it in small portions. It should be creamy in colour, cool to the touch and easy to break. It will keep for 4–5 days stored in a polythene bag in the refrigerator, and can be frozen for up to 6 months.

☞ Dried yeast is more convenient as it is readily available in supermarkets. Keep it no longer than 6 months.

☞ Easy-blend yeast is a quick-acting dried yeast, with added improvers which activate the yeast more quickly. It is stirred directly into the dry ingredients, not reconstituted with water. It will keep for up to 6 months in a cool place.

☞ Strong plain flour is needed for yeast baking because it develops quickly into an elastic dough and gives better results than ordinary flours.

☞ Sugar is the food that yeast needs in order to grow. Sometimes sugar is added to dried yeast to get it working.

☞ Fat is used in yeast baking to enrich doughs, delay staling, and improve the quality of the cake.

☞ Liquid for mixing a dough must be at blood heat. If it is any warmer, it can kill off the yeast, and the dough will not rise at all. To test for blood heat, dab a few drops of the liquid on your wrist. If it feels warm, the liquid is too hot.

PREPARING THE YEAST LIQUID

Fresh yeast should be creamed with some of the liquid from the recipe. Dried yeast needs reconstituting: put about 150ml/¼ pint of the measured liquid into a jug, stir in the sugar and sprinkle over the dried yeast. Leave this in a warm place until frothy, about 15 minutes. Dried yeast works more slowly than fresh so allow a little extra time for rising.

KNEADING

Kneading strengthens and develops the gluten in the dough, so that you get a good rise. Use only enough flour on the work surface to prevent the dough from sticking. Knead by folding the dough towards you, then pushing down and away from you with the heels of your hands. Give a quarter turn, fold and push away, developing a rocking motion. Knead for about 10 minutes or until the dough feels firm and elastic and is no longer sticky.

USING A MIXER OR PROCESSOR

A table-top electric mixer with a dough hook attachment is ideal for kneading dough. (Smaller mixers cannot cope with the power needed to handle dough.) Food processors fitted with a plastic blunt blade can knead small amounts of dough, but it is still advisable to knead by hand a little afterwards to get a really smooth dough.

Danish pastry shapes:

Tivolis

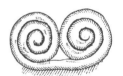

Chocolate pinwheels

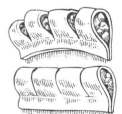

Cockscombs

Windmills

$\mathcal{S}$TOLLEN

In Germany, Christmas Eve is a day of feasting and real celebration and the 25th is a quieter family celebration. Stollen fruit bread first became popular in Dresden, but now it is made all over Germany for the Christmas season. Make extra for friends and wrap the bread in red ribbons to contrast with the white sugar.

YEAST BATTER:
2 TSP YEAST AND
½ TSP CASTER SUGAR,
OR 15 G/½ OZ FRESH YEAST
6 TBSP MILK, AT BLOOD HEAT
50 G/2 OZ STRONG PLAIN
WHITE FLOUR
DOUGH:
175 G/6 OZ STRONG PLAIN
WHITE FLOUR
½ TSP SALT
25 G/1 OZ CASTER SUGAR

25 G/1 OZ BUTTER
1 EGG, SIZE 3, BEATEN
25 G/1 OZ FLAKED ALMONDS
GRATED ZEST 1 LEMON
50 G/2 OZ CURRANTS
50 G/2 OZ SULTANAS
25 G/1 OZ CHOPPED CANDIED
MIXED PEEL
25 G/1 OZ BUTTER, MELTED
50 G/2 OZ GLACÉ CHERRIES,
RINSED, DRIED AND HALVED
ICING SUGAR, TO DREDGE

1 To make the yeast batter, stir the dried yeast and sugar into the milk and leave for 5 minutes, or blend the fresh yeast into the milk. Mix in the flour and leave in a warm place until frothy; this should take about 20 minutes.

2 Sift the flour and salt into a bowl and stir in the sugar, then rub in the butter until it resembles fine crumbs. Make a well in the middle, add the egg and the yeast batter and mix to a soft dough. Turn on to a floured surface and knead until smooth. Return to the bowl, cover with oiled polythene and leave to rise until doubled in size, about 1 hour.

3 Grease a baking sheet. Place the dough on the floured surface and knead lightly to knock out the air. Press the almonds, zest, currants, sultanas and peel into the dough and knead until well mixed in.

4 Roll out the dough to a round 25cm/10inches in diameter. Brush the surface with the melted butter, then spread the cherries in a strip across the centre. Fold the dough over into three to cover the cherries. Place on the baking sheet, brush with melted butter and cover with the oiled polythene again. Leave to prove until light and puffy, about 30 minutes.

5 Set the oven to 200°C/400°F/Gas 6. Bake towards the top of the oven for about 35 minutes, until golden, then cool on a wire rack. Dredge heavily with icing sugar when cold. Serve sliced and buttered.

VARIATION: *Omit the cherries and add 75g/3oz of almond paste (see page 160), rolled into a sausage shape. Place along the centre of the dough, fold over and bake as above.*

TO FREEZE: *Wrap in foil. Keeps for 5 months.*

Illustrated opposite page 144

*P*ANETTONE

Panettone is an Italian cake made in Milan. It is usually sold, in festive boxes, in delicatessens around Christmas. Make your own version for a fraction of the cost of a bought one – it is a nice light alternative to all the rich foods of the festive season.

- 350 G/12 OZ STRONG PLAIN WHITE FLOUR
- ¼ TSP GROUND NUTMEG
- 20 G/¾ OZ FRESH YEAST
- 225 ML/8 FL OZ MILK, AT BLOOD HEAT
- 150 G/5 OZ BUTTER, AT ROOM TEMPERATURE
- 2 EGG YOLKS, SIZE 3

- 50 G/2 OZ SOFT BROWN SUGAR
- 100 G/4 OZ CHOPPED CANDIED MIXED PEEL
- 75 G/3 OZ SULTANAS
- FINELY GRATED ZEST ½ LEMON
- BEATEN EGG YOLK OR MILK, TO GLAZE
- ICING SUGAR, TO DREDGE

1 Grease an 18cm/7inch round deep cake tin and line with a double band of greased greaseproof paper to come 10cm/4inches higher than the rim of the tin. Secure the join with a paper clip. Or grease a deep kugelhupf mould.

2 Sift the flour and nutmeg into a large bowl and make a well in the centre. Blend the yeast with the milk until dissolved, then pour into the flour. Gradually draw in the flour from the sides and mix together well to make a soft dough. Cover the bowl with a clean cloth and leave to rise in a warm place until the dough is doubled in size, about 1 hour.

3 Turn out the dough on to a floured surface or into a table-top electric mixer with a dough hook. Knead to knock out the air, until the dough is smooth, then gradually mix in the butter in pieces followed by the egg yolks. Gently mix in the sugar, peel, sultanas and zest until well combined.

4 Cover with a cloth and leave to rise for 45 minutes or until doubled in size. Place the dough in the tin, and leave to rise again until it reaches halfway up the paper lining or fills the kugelhupf mould and looks puffy.

5 Set the oven to 200°C/400°F/Gas 6. Cut a cross right through the dough. Brush the surface with beaten egg yolk or milk and bake for 20 minutes, then turn down the oven temperature to 180°C/350°F/Gas 4 and bake for a further 30–40 minutes or until a skewer inserted in the centre comes out clean.

6 Leave the cake to cool in the tin for 10 minutes, then turn out on to a wire rack to cool completely. Dust with sifted icing sugar when cold. Eat within 5 days.

TO FREEZE: *Wrap in foil. Keeps for 2 months.*

RIGHT (from top to bottom): Black Bun (see page 101); Dundee Cake (see page 98); Stollen (see page 142).

DANISH PASTRIES

MAKES 8 OF EACH VARIETY

- 550 G/1 ¼ LB STRONG PLAIN WHITE FLOUR
- ½ TSP SALT
- 275 G/10 OZ BUTTER
- 1 7 G SACHET EASY-BLEND DRIED YEAST
- 75 G/3 OZ CASTER SUGAR
- 175ML/6 FLOZ WATER, AT BLOOD HEAT

- 2 EGGS, SIZE 3, BEATEN
- 1 EGG WHITE, TO GLAZE
- **DECORATION:**
- GLACÉ ICING, MADE WITH 175 G/6 OZ ICING SUGAR AND 1 TSP LEMON JUICE (SEE PAGE 166)
- GLACÉ CHERRIES OR FLAKED ALMONDS

1 Sift the flour and salt into a large bowl. Cut 50g/2oz butter into small pieces and rub into the flour until it resembles crumbs. Stir in the yeast and sugar, then mix in the water and eggs to make a soft dough.

2 Turn on to a lightly floured surface and knead for 5 minutes or until smooth and elastic. Place the dough in an oiled polythene bag and chill in the refrigerator for 15 minutes. Cut the remaining butter into sixteen slices and chill these on a plate.

3 Cut the dough in half, and roll out each half into a rectangle 38 × 20cm/15 × 8inches. Arrange four slices of chilled butter evenly in the centre of each rectangle.

4 Fold one-third of each dough rectangle over to the centre to cover the butter slices, and press down lightly to seal. Put four more slices on top of the folded dough, then fold over the remaining plain third to cover. Press the edges to seal.

5 Give each piece of dough a half turn and roll out to a strip 40 × 15cm/16 × 6 inches. Fold the ends to meet in the centre, then fold over in half again. Cover both pieces with oiled polythene, and chill in the refrigerator for 30 minutes.

6 Repeat the last step twice more, chilling for at least 2 hours, then divide each piece of dough in half and roll out as needed (see the options given on page 146).

7 Place the shaped pastries on a baking sheet and leave to rise for 20–30 minutes.

8 Set the oven to 200°C/400°F/Gas 6. Glaze the pastries with egg white, then bake for 10 minutes. Reduce the oven temperature to 180°C/350°F/Gas 4 and bake for a further 15 minutes. Leave to cool on the baking sheets.

9 When the pastries are cold, decorate them with glacé icing and glacé cherries or flaked almonds.

TO FREEZE: *Wrap dough in freezer bag or foil. Thaw overnight in refrigerator or for 6 hours at room temperature, then shape, fill and bake as required. Keeps for 1 month.*

LEFT (from top to bottom): Chelsea Buns (see page 152); Danish Pastries (see above); Hot Cross Buns (see page 148).

WINDMILLS

Mix 6 tbsp ground almonds with 2 tbsp lemon curd. Roll out one-quarter of the dough into a rectangle 15 × 30cm/6 × 12 inches. Cut into eight 7.5cm/3inch squares. Make diagonal cuts from each corner to within 1cm/½inch of the centre. Place a knob of filling in the centre of each square. Starting clockwise, fold each left-hand top corner to the centre and press to seal. Decorate each baked pastry with a halved glacé cherry.

TIVOLIS

Mix 50g/2oz butter, at room temperature, 1 tbsp demerara sugar, 2 tsp ground cinnamon and 100g/4oz no-need-to-soak dried apricots, chopped. Roll out one-quarter of the dough into a rectangle 15 × 30cm/6 × 12inches. Cut into eight 7.5cm/3inch squares. Spread a little filling diagonally over each square from corner to corner. Half turn the square so it is diamond-shaped. Make a small slit in the near corner of the dough. Fold edge A over filling to the centre. Lift the top corner B to centre and push it through the slit piece to seal.

CHOCOLATE PINWHEELS

Melt 100g/4oz plain chocolate with 1 tbsp coffee essence, then stir in 2 tbsp chopped toasted hazelnuts. Roll out one-quarter of the dough to a 30cm/12inch square. Cut into eight strips each 30 × 4.5cm/12 × 1½inches. Spread a little filling along each and roll up the two long ends towards the middle. Press together to seal then turn on to one side and flatten out with the palm of your hand. Decorate baked pastries with flaked almonds.

COCKSCOMBS

Peel, core and slice 1 large Cox's apple and cook to a pulp with 1 tsp lemon juice and a knob of butter. Stir in 25g/1oz sultanas and 1 tsp mixed spice, cook for 1 minute longer and leave to cool. Roll out one-quarter of the dough into a rectangle 15 × 30cm/6 × 12inches. Cut into eight 7.5cm/3inch squares. Spread the apple filling over half of each square to within 1cm/½inch of the edges. Fold over in half and slit the folded edge in three places. Curve round slightly to open out. Decorate the baked pastries with flaked almonds.

$\mathcal{B}$ATH BUNS

MAKES 12

These buns were prescribed by an eighteenth-century physician,
Dr Oliver, who sent his patients to Bath to take the waters.
The buns were so rich and delicious that the patients often ate
more than was good for them, and were then put on to Dr Oliver's
regime of slimming yet nourishing Bath Oliver Biscuits. I think
I prefer the buns.

- 675 G/1 ½ LB STRONG PLAIN WHITE FLOUR
- 1 TSP SALT
- 75 G/3 OZ BUTTER
- 75 G/3 OZ CASTER SUGAR
- 1 7G SACHET EASY-BLEND DRIED YEAST
- 2 EGGS, SIZE 3
- 150 ML/¼ PINT PLAIN YOGURT

- 300 ML/½ PINT WATER, AT BLOOD HEAT
- 175 G/6 OZ DRIED MIXED FRUIT
- MILK, TO GLAZE
- 25 G/1 OZ SUGAR NIBS, LUMP SUGAR OR PRESERVING SUGAR
- 2 TBSP GOLDEN SYRUP

1 Sift the flour and salt into a bowl and rub in the butter until the mixture resembles fine crumbs. Stir in the caster sugar and yeast. Beat the eggs, yogurt and water together, then pour into the dry mixture. Mix to a sticky dough and knead for 5 minutes or until smooth.

2 Replace the dough in the bowl and cover with oiled polythene. Leave in a warm place to rise for about 1 hour or until the dough is doubled in size.

3 Grease one large or two small baking sheets. Turn out the dough on to a floured surface and knead to knock out the air, until the dough is smooth and elastic again. Knead in the dried fruit. Cut into twelve equal pieces and roll each into a round. Place well apart on the baking sheet and cover with oiled polythene. Leave to rise for 30 minutes until doubled in size.

4 Set the oven to 190°C/375°F/Gas 5. Brush the tops of the buns with milk and sprinkle over the sugar nibs. Bake for 35 minutes or until firm and brown. Leave on the sheet to cool, then brush with golden syrup for a sticky glaze.

5 Pull the buns apart and serve split and buttered.

TO FREEZE: *Wrap in freezer bags, removing all air. Keeps for 3 months.*

Hot Cross Buns

MAKES A BAKER'S DOZEN (13)

These sweet and sticky buns are a traditional treat for Good Friday,
served split and spread with plenty of butter.

- 450 G/1 LB STRONG PLAIN
  WHITE FLOUR
- PINCH SALT
- 50 G/2 OZ BUTTER
- 17 G SACHET EASY-BLEND
  DRIED YEAST
- 50 G/2 OZ DARK
  MUSCOVADO SUGAR
- 2 TSP MIXED SPICE
- 100 G/4 OZ CURRANTS

- 50 G/2 OZ CHOPPED CANDIED
  MIXED PEEL
- 150 ML/¼ PINT MILK,
  AT BLOOD HEAT
- 1 EGG, SIZE 3, BEATEN
- **GLAZE:**
- 40 G/1½ OZ CASTER SUGAR
- 4 TBSP MILK
- **CROSSES:**
- 2 TBSP STRONG WHITE FLOUR
  OR SHORTCRUST PASTRY SCRAPS

1 Sift the flour and salt into a bowl and rub in the butter until it resembles fine crumbs. Stir in the yeast, sugar, mixed spice, fruit and peel.

2 Make a well in the centre and pour in the milk, 6 tbsp lukewarm water and the beaten egg. Mix thoroughly into a dough.

3 Turn on to a lightly floured surface and knead for about 10 minutes or until smooth and very elastic. Alternatively, knead the dough in a food processor with a plastic blade for 30 seconds, or in a table-top mixer with a dough hook for 2–3 minutes.

4 Oil two baking sheets. Divide the dough into thirteen pieces and shape each piece into a smooth round. Place on the baking sheets, spaced well apart. Cover loosely with oiled polythene and leave in a warm place to rise until doubled in size. This should take 1 hour.

5 Set the oven to 200°C/400°F/Gas 6. Mix 2 tsp of the caster sugar and 2 tbsp of milk together for the first glaze. Remove the oiled polythene and gently brush the buns with the glaze.

6 To make the crosses, mix the flour with 2 tbsp water to make a smooth paste. Place in a greaseproof paper piping bag (see page 182) and snip a small hole in the end. Pipe a cross on each bun. Alternatively, roll out shortcrust pastry scraps, cut into thin strips and place on the buns in the shape of a cross.

7 Bake the buns for 20 minutes or until dark golden and hollow sounding when tapped on the base.

8 Gently heat the remaining sugar with the rest of the milk until dissolved, then boil for 3 minutes. Place the buns on a wire rack and brush with the glaze while still warm. Leave to cool completely.

TO FREEZE: *Freeze unglazed buns in a rigid container. Keeps for 5 months. Thaw at room temperature and refresh in a warm oven.*

ALTERNATIVELY: *Freeze the unrisen, unbaked buns on their baking sheets. Keeps for up to 3 months. Thaw at room temperature for 3–4 hours and allow time for rising.*

Illustrated opposite page 145

ℒARDY CAKE

Lardy cake is rich and sticky, and definitely not for dieters. Serve it upside-down, to show the delicious toffee-like layer which forms underneath.

1 TSP DRIED YEAST AND ½ TSP CASTER SUGAR, OR 7 G/¼ OZ FRESH YEAST	**FILLING:** 100 G/4 OZ LARD
150ML/¼ PINT MIXED MILK AND WATER, AT BLOOD HEAT	100 G/4 OZ SOFT LIGHT BROWN SUGAR
225 G/8 OZ STRONG PLAIN WHITE FLOUR	175 G/6 OZ MIXED DRIED FRUIT
½ TSP SALT	1 TSP MIXED SPICE
25 G/1 OZ LARD	

Fold dough into thirds, roll and repeat

Roll out filled dough to fit tin, and mark diagonally

1 Stir the dried yeast and sugar into the liquid and leave for 15 minutes until frothy, or blend the fresh yeast into the liquid. Sift the flour and salt into a bowl and rub in the lard. Add the yeast liquid and mix to a soft dough.

2 Turn on to a floured surface and knead until smooth and elastic. Return to the bowl, cover with oiled polythene and leave the dough to rise until doubled in size, about 1¼ hours.

3 Turn out the risen dough and knock out the air. Roll out to an oblong 1cm/½inch thick. Place one-third of the lard in small dots over the top two-thirds of the dough and sprinkle with one-third of the sugar, fruit and spice. Fold the uncovered dough up and the top third down over it. Give the dough a quarter turn, then roll out to an oblong again. Repeat the rolling and folding twice more, using up the remaining filling ingredients.

4 Grease a 20 × 25cm/8 × 10inch roasting tin. Roll out the dough to fit the tin, then cover and leave to prove until light and puffy, about 1 hour.

5 Set the oven to 220°C/425°F/Gas 7. Bake for about 40 minutes or until golden brown. Leave to cool in the tin, to let the cake absorb the fat as it cools. Serve upside-down, sliced.

TO FREEZE: *Wrap in freezer bags or foil. Keeps for 3 months.*

CORNISH SAFFRON CAKE

- ½ TSP SAFFRON STRANDS
- 4 TSP DRIED YEAST AND
  ¼ TSP CASTER SUGAR,
  OR 25 G/1 OZ FRESH YEAST
- 150ML/¼ PINT MILK,
  AT BLOOD HEAT
- 450 G/1 LB STRONG PLAIN
  WHITE FLOUR

- 1 TSP SALT
- 100 G/4 OZ BUTTER
- FINELY GRATED ZEST
  ½ LEMON
- 25 G/1 OZ SOFT BROWN SUGAR
- 175 G/6 OZ CURRANTS OR
  MIXED DRIED FRUIT

1 Place the saffron in a bowl and pour over 150ml/¼ pint boiling water. Leave to infuse and cool for about 2 hours. Grease a 20cm/8inch round deep cake tin.

2 Stir the dried yeast and sugar into the milk and leave for 15 minutes until frothy, or blend the fresh yeast into the milk.

3 Sift the flour and salt into a bowl and rub in the butter until it resembles fine crumbs. Stir in the lemon zest and sugar. Strain in the saffron infusion and add the yeast liquid. Beat well, with a table-top electric mixer if possible, then mix in the fruit. Place the dough in the tin and leave to rise in a warm place until the dough is puffy and reaches the top of the tin.

4 Set the oven to 200°C/400°F/Gas 6. Bake for 30 minutes, then turn down the oven temperature to 180°C/350°F/Gas 4 and bake for a further 20–30 minutes or until golden on top and hollow-sounding when tapped on the base.

5 Turn out to cool on a wire rack, and serve sliced and buttered.

TO FREEZE: *Wrap in foil. Keeps for 3 months.*

CHELSEA BUNS

MAKES 9

*King George the Third and Queen Charlotte used to travel to
the Old Chelsea Bun House and eat these buns in public on
Sunday afternoons.*

YEAST BATTER:
- 2 TSP DRIED YEAST AND
  1 TSP CASTER SUGAR,
  OR 15 G/½ OZ FRESH YEAST
- 5 TBSP MILK, AT BLOOD HEAT
- 50 G/2 OZ STRONG PLAIN
  WHITE FLOUR

DOUGH:
- 175 G/6 OZ STRONG PLAIN
  WHITE FLOUR
- ½ TSP SALT
- 25 G/1 OZ CASTER SUGAR

- 25 G/1 OZ BUTTER
- 1 EGG, BEATEN

FILLING:
- 15 G/½ OZ BUTTER, MELTED
- 100 G/4 OZ MIXED DRIED FRUIT
- 25 G/1 OZ CHOPPED CANDIED
  MIXED PEEL
- 1 TSP GROUND CINNAMON
- 50 G/2 OZ DARK MUSCOVADO
  SUGAR
- GOLDEN SYRUP, TO GLAZE

*Sprinkle filling over dough,
and roll up*

*Cut along length into
nine slices*

1 To make the yeast batter, stir the dried yeast and sugar into the milk and leave for 5 minutes, or blend the fresh yeast into the milk. Stir in the flour and leave in a warm place for about 20 minutes until frothy.

2 For the dough, mix the flour, salt and sugar together in a bowl. Rub in the butter, then mix in the egg and yeast batter to make a soft dough. Place on a well-floured surface and knead until smooth and no longer sticky. Return to the bowl, cover with oiled polythene and leave to rise in a warm place until doubled in size. This should take about 1 hour. Grease a 18–20cm/7–8inch square tin.

3 Place the risen dough on the floured surface and knead to knock out the air. Roll out into a rectangle 30 × 23cm/12 × 9inches. Brush the surface of the dough with the melted butter. Mix the fruit, peel, cinnamon and sugar together and sprinkle over the butter. Roll up from a long side and cut across into 9 equal slices. Place the slices, cut side down, close together in the tin. Cover and leave to prove until doubled in size, about 40 minutes.

4 Set the oven to 220°C/425°F/Gas 7. Remove the polythene and bake for 20–25 minutes until golden brown. Turn out on to a wire rack to cool, then brush with golden syrup to give a sticky glaze. Pull the buns apart to serve.

TO FREEZE: *Wrap in freezer bags. Keeps for 3 months.*

Illustrated opposite page 145

BABAS WITH RUM AND HONEY SYRUP

MAKES 12

- **YEAST BATTER:**
- 2 TSP DRIED YEAST AND 1 TSP CASTER SUGAR, OR 15 G/½ OZ FRESH YEAST
- 5 TBSP MILK, AT BLOOD HEAT
- 25 G/1 OZ STRONG PLAIN WHITE FLOUR
- **DOUGH:**
- 150 G/5 OZ STRONG PLAIN WHITE FLOUR
- LARGE PINCH SALT
- 1 TBSP CASTER SUGAR

- 75 G/3 OZ BUTTER
- 3 EGGS, SIZE 3, BEATEN
- 75 G/3 OZ CURRANTS
- FINELY GRATED ZEST ½ LEMON
- **RUM AND HONEY SYRUP:**
- 8 TBSP CLEAR HONEY
- RUM TO TASTE
- **TO FINISH:**
- APRICOT GLAZE (SEE PAGE 169)
- 300 ML/½ PINT DOUBLE OR WHIPPING CREAM, WHIPPED

1 To make the yeast batter, stir the dried yeast and sugar into the milk and leave for 5 minutes, or blend the fresh yeast with the milk. Mix in the flour and leave in a warm place until frothy, about 20 minutes.

2 Lightly grease twelve 9cm/3½inch ring or baba moulds, or use flan tins or dariole moulds.

3 Sift the flour, salt and sugar into a bowl. Rub in the butter, then add the eggs, currants, zest and yeast batter. Beat well with a wooden spoon for 3–4 minutes.

4 Half fill the prepared moulds with the dough. Cover and leave to rise for about 25 minutes, until the tins are two-thirds full.

5 Set the oven to 200°C/400°F/Gas 6. Bake for 10–15 minutes until golden brown. Cool in the moulds for a few minutes.

6 Make the syrup while the babas are baking: warm all the syrup ingredients together with 8 tbsp water. Spoon the syrup over each cake while they are still warm. Leave to cool, in the moulds, on a wire rack.

7 Brush each cake with apricot glaze when cold and pipe on a whirl of cream.

TO FREEZE: *Wrap baked unsoaked babas in foil. Keeps for 1 month. Thaw, soak in syrup and decorate.*

SAVARIN

Make up the baba dough (see page 153), omitting the currants. Grease a 20cm/8inch ring mould or kugelhupf mould and spoon in the dough. Cover and leave to rise until the mixture almost reaches the top of the tin, about 30–40 minutes.

Bake at 200°C/400°F/Gas 6 for 20–30 minutes or until golden brown and springy to the touch. Leave to cool in the tin for 5 minutes, then turn out on to a wire rack placed over a tray and prick with a fine skewer. Paint with the rum and honey syrup, or substitute Kirsch for the rum. When cold, brush with apricot glaze, and decorate with large pieces of glacé fruit or fill the centre with fresh fruit. Freeze as for babas.

$\mathcal{W}$H A T W E N T W R O N G ?

Baking with yeast can be more complicated than ordinary baking. If you have encountered problems with baking with yeast, the following tips may be of help:

☞ THE DOUGH COLLAPSES WHEN IT IS PUT IN THE OVEN:
This happens when the dough has been left to prove for too long.

☞ THE CAKE HAS A COARSE, OPEN TEXTURE:
This can be caused by adding too much liquid, baking in too cool an oven, or over-proving.

☞ THE CAKE HAS LARGE HOLES IN IT:
This happens when the dough is not knocked back properly, causing large air bubbles to remain in it.

☞ THEERE IS A SOUR, YEASTY SMELL TO THE CAKE:
This happens when too much yeast is used, and is also caused by over-proving.

☞ THE CAKE HAS A CLOSE, HEAVY TEXTURE AND DID NOT RISE SUFFICIENTLY:
This will happen when too much salt is added, or the wrong flour is used, i.e., ordinary soft flour, not strong flour. It can also happen when the dough has not been kneaded or proved sufficiently, or if the yeast has actually been killed off by rising in too hot a place.

☞ THE CAKE STALES QUICKLY AND BECOMES CRUMBLY:
Again this can be caused by the addition of too much yeast, so measure it out carefully. Use of soft flour can also cause this, as can rising too quickly in too warm a place, or not rising enough.

*I*CINGS AND FILLINGS

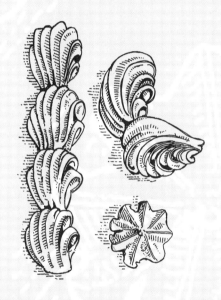

The plainest of cakes can be made that little bit more special with a quick and simple icing or filling. The more elaborate the decoration, however, the more eye-catching and appealing the cake appears.

Almond paste, royal and fondant icings can all be used to create impressive effects for special occasion cakes, and with skill and practice you really can produce amazing results. Those sticky items of pâtissèrie that we often see in continental cake shops are often covered in sophisticated coatings, such as crème au beurre or praline. These delicious toppings are not so difficult to make, and can be produced easily at home with a little extra care to help simple cakes look expensive.

If you need to whip up a children's party cake quickly, it is very easy to make a plain buttercream and cover it in minutes. Add a few sweets and novelties and the cake's complete. Once you have tried the chocolate fudge icing or seven-minute frosting, you will realize it doesn't take long to decorate a cake, and you'll be the most popular person around. Life just wouldn't be the same without the occasional gooey piece of cake, would it?

ALMOND PASTE

MAKES 450G/1LB

Almond paste is used to cover cakes that are going to be finished with royal icing or fondant icing. The layer of almond paste seals in the cake underneath, keeping it moist, and provides a good flat surface to decorate. Any minor disasters such as broken or tilting cakes can be rectified or repaired with almond paste, before decorating. You can also use almond paste for making decorative tops as in Simnel cake (see page 102), or for modelling animals, flowers and shapes. Colour it only with paste food colours, as liquid food colouring will alter the consistency, especially if used in large amounts.

There are some excellent ready-made brands of almond paste on the market, and some of these will actually work out cheaper to use if you are covering a large cake. Home-made almond paste has a wonderful texture and flavour of its own, and, of course, contains no additives like colourings or preservatives. The ready-made white almond paste now on sale is a good alternative, however, and sometimes works out to be more economical. Only buy the yellow type for decorative purposes as this can show through icings or cause staining. Staining of royal icing, in particular, can occur if the almond paste has not been allowed to dry out sufficiently or home-made paste has been over-kneaded, bringing out the oil from the almonds.

The almonds given in the chart show how much almond paste is needed to cover cakes of different sizes. Store made-up or opened packs of almond paste, wrapped tightly in polythene, for up to 3 weeks in the refrigerator, or keep scraps, useful for patching, or modelling, in a polythene bag in the freezer. Always roll out the almond paste on a surface dusted with icing or caster sugar; never be tempted to use cornflour, as this will ferment underneath the cake. See page 176 for how to cover a cake with almond paste.

- 100 G/4 OZ ICING SUGAR
- 100 G/4 OZ CASTER SUGAR (PREFERABLY STORED WITH A VANILLA POD)
- 225 G/8 OZ GROUND ALMONDS
- 1 EGG, SIZE 3
- 1 TSP LEMON JUICE
- 1 TBSP BRANDY OR SHERRY
- 1 DROP VANILLA ESSENCE

1 Sift the sugars and almonds into a bowl. Whisk the remaining ingredients together, then mix into the dry mixture. Knead well until the paste is smooth.

2 Wrap in cling film and keep in a cool place until needed. The paste can be made 2–3 days before use, but after that it will start to dry out and be difficult to handle.

NOTE: *To make a white almond paste, use 2 egg whites instead of 1 whole egg.*

RIGHT (from top to bottom): Devil's Food Cake (see page 42); Rich Chocolate and Almond Layer Cake (see page 46); Decadent Chocolate Roulade (see page 43).

QUANTITY GUIDE
FOR ALMOND PASTE

TO COVER TOP AND SIDES OF A CAKE

Round Tin	Square Tin	Almond Paste
15cm/6inches	12.5cm/5inches	350g/12oz
18cm/7inches	15cm/6inches	450g/1lb
20cm/8inches	18cm/7inches	675g/1½lb
23cm/9inches	20cm/8inches	800g/1¾lb
25cm/10inches	23cm/9inches	900g/2lb
28cm/11inches	25cm/10inches	1kg/2¼lb
30cm/12inches	28cm/11inches	1.1kg/2½lb
33cm/13inches	30cm/12inches	1.4kg/3lb
35cm/14inches	33cm/13inches	1.6kg/3½lb

BOILED ALMOND PASTE

MAKES 450G/1LB

*This type of almond paste can be iced over almost immediately, and
needs less time to dry out. This is useful if you ever have to ice a cake
in a real hurry, or are worried about eating uncooked eggs, which
bind the paste. You will need a sugar thermometer to ensure
accurate results.*

- 225 G/8 OZ GRANULATED SUGAR
- PINCH CREAM OF TARTAR
- 175 G/6 OZ GROUND ALMONDS

- 1 EGG WHITE, SIZE 3
- 75 G/3 OZ ICING SUGAR,
  SIFTED

1 Place the granulated sugar and 5 tbsp water in a heavy-based saucepan and
dissolve over a low heat. When every grain has dissolved, bring to boiling point, add
the cream of tartar and boil to 116°C/240°F.

Continued overleaf

LEFT: Child's 'Number'
Cake (see page 186).

2 Remove from the heat and stir rapidly until the syrup begins to turn cloudy. Add the ground almonds. Whisk the egg white lightly and add to the mixture. Return to a low heat and cook for 2 minutes, stirring constantly.

3 Pour on to a marble slab or clean heatproof surface. Work in the icing sugar using a palette knife, lifting the edges of the mixture and bringing it into the centre. When the mixture is cool enough to handle, knead it well. If the paste is too sticky, add a little more icing sugar. Wrap in foil until needed.

R OYAL ICING

Royal icing is simply a paste made from icing sugar and egg whites.
Glycerine can be added during mixing to soften it for covering
cakes, and lemon juice added to harden it for detailed piping work
or for the first coating of a wedding cake that has to support heavy
tiers. Adding a tiny dot of blue colouring will make the icing look
whiter, but don't overdo this as it can easily turn to grey.

CONSISTENCY

The problem most cooks have with royal icing is that of using the wrong consistency. For example, if you make the icing for piping too stiff it will be difficult to work with and you will end up with an aching arm. Make the basic recipe thicker or thinner according to the use you are putting it to.

Cover the cake with two or more thin coats of icing, each progressively thinner than the last. For the first coat, the icing should stand up in peaks when the spoon is pulled away. Do not add glycerine to the icing to cover the base of a wedding cake, as this is the layer that will take most weight.

Make icing for piping of a firmer consistency, with added lemon juice, particularly for trellis work. Icing for run-out work should be very thin. It is a good idea to beat all icing to the consistency of thick cream, then add more sugar gradually until you are happy with the feel of the icing.

Under-beating is the reason for the jaw-breaking royal icing we've all eaten on Christmas cakes. Well-beaten icing is also easier to handle as well. See page 177 for how to cover a cake with royal icing.

SUGAR

Always sift the icing sugar before mixing. It is extremely frustrating if you find a lump of unsifted sugar blocking a nozzle and halting the flow of icing. Old sugar, or sugar that has become damp, can be lumpy and gritty, so sift this two or three times. Always use a nylon sieve, as specks of metal can come away from metal sieves and fleck the icing.

Egg whites used for royal icing must be perfectly fresh, and untainted by odours from strong foods stored in the refrigerator. When separating eggs, take care not to let any yolk get into the whites. If this happens, use the egg for cooking and start again, otherwise the icing will have a yellow tinge and heavy consistency. Be sure to remove all specks of membrane too. Dried egg whites give excellent results for icing and can be stored for long periods in the cupboard; they are simply reconstituted with water according to the packet instructions.

$\mathcal{Q}$UANTITY GUIDE
FOR ROYAL ICING

TO COVER TOP AND SIDES OF A CAKE

Round Cake	Square Cake	Royal Icing
(weight of sugar)		
15cm/6inches	12.5cm/5inches	450g/1lb
18cm/7inches	15cm/6inches	550g/1¼lb
20cm/8inches	18cm/7inches	700g/1½lb
23cm/9inches	20cm/8inches	900g/2lb
25cm/10inches	23cm/9inches	1kg/2¼lb
28cm/11inches	25cm/10inches	1.1kg/2½lb
30cm/12inches	28cm/11inches	1.4kg/3lb
33cm/13inches	30cm/12inches	1.6kg/3½lb
35cm/14inches	33cm/13inches	1.8kg/4lb

$\mathcal{F}$ONDANT ICING

MAKES 675G/1 ½LB

Fondant or sugar paste icing is something of a newcomer to cake decoration. It was developed in hot, humid countries, where royal icing just refused to set. Its popularity has really grown as it can be used so quickly and easily; just roll it out like pastry and smooth it over the cake. It is a wonderful medium for modelling frills, flowers and small animals, too.

Fondant can be made at home or purchased ready-made. The home-made variety contains liquid glucose, which is available in tubs from chemists' shops. See page 179 for how to cover a cake with fondant icing.

- 675 G/1 ½LB ICING SUGAR, SIFTED
- 2 EGG WHITES, SIZE 3
- 2 TBSP LIQUID GLUCOSE

- 1 TSP GLYCERINE
- FEW DROPS ROSEWATER (OPTIONAL)

1 Sift the icing sugar into a large, grease-free, dry bowl and make a well in the centre. Add the remaining ingredients to the well and gradually blend into the sugar with the fingertips.

2 Knead together until smooth, then roll up the paste into a ball. The paste should be smooth and easy to roll. If sticky, knead in a little more sugar until manageable. Keep in a thick polythene bag until needed.

$\mathcal{B}$OILED FONDANT ICING

COVERS 12–16 FANCIES OR A 20 CM (8") ROUND CAKE

This fondant is poured over cakes, particularly small ones like fancies.

- 450 G/1 LB GRANULATED SUGAR
- 1 TBSP LIQUID GLUCOSE

1 Place 150ml/¼ pint water and the sugar in a heavy-based saucepan and gently heat until the sugar has completely dissolved. Bring to the boil slowly, then add the liquid glucose.

2 Boil until the syrup reaches 115°C/240°F on a sugar thermometer. Remove from the heat and when the liquid stops bubbling, pour it into two heatproof bowls. Leave to cool until a skin forms.

3 Beat one half with a wooden spoon until the liquid becomes thick and white and turns into a solid mass. Place on a clean surface and knead with your fingers until smooth. Repeat with the other half of the mixture.

4 Break the fondant into large lumps and smooth into balls. Store in an airtight container until needed. The icing will keep for 2 months in the refrigerator.

5 To use, take four pieces at a time for small cakes and place in a heatproof bowl set over a pan of hot water. Heat gently until a thick, coating consistency is reached. If too thick, thin down with a little hot water. Beat in colourings.

6 Pour over apricot-glazed or almond-pasted cakes. Smooth on with a palette knife, covering any gaps immediately, then leave to set.

QUANTITY GUIDE
FOR FONDANT ICING

TO COVER TOP AND SIDES OF A CAKE

Round Cake	Square Cake	Fondant Icing
15cm/6inches	12.5cm/5inches	350g/12oz
18cm/7inches	15cm/6inches	450g/1lb
20cm/8inches	18cm/7inches	675g/1½lb
23cm/9inches	20cm/8inches	800g/1¾lb
25cm/10inches	23cm/9inches	900g/2lb
28cm/11inches	25cm/10inches	1kg/2¼lb
30cm/12inches	28cm/11inches	1.1kg/2½lb
33cm/13inches	30cm/12inches	1.4kg/3lb
35cm/14inches	33cm/13inches	1.6kg/3½lb

$\mathcal{S}$EVEN-MINUTE FROSTING

COVERS A 20CM (8") ROUND CAKE

- 1 EGG WHITE, SIZE 2
- 175 G/6 OZ CASTER SUGAR
- PINCH SALT
- PINCH CREAM OF TARTAR

1 Place all the ingredients with 2 tbsp water in a large grease-free heatproof bowl and whisk until foamy. Set the bowl over a saucepan of boiling water and whisk until the mixture forms soft peaks – this should take about 7 minutes.

2 Use to cover the cake immediately, smoothing and swirling on with a palette knife. The frosting will set as it cools.

VARIATIONS:
LEMON: *Beat in 1 tsp lemon juice before the frosting thickens.*
BUTTERSCOTCH: *Substitute demerara sugar for white sugar.*
COFFEE: *Beat in 1 tsp liquid coffee essence before the frosting thickens.*

$\mathcal{G}$LACÉ ICING

COVERS 12 CUP CAKES OR TOP OF A 20CM (8") ROUND CAKE

- 100 G/4 OZ ICING SUGAR
- LIQUID FOOD COLOURING (OPTIONAL)

1 Sift the icing sugar into a bowl and gradually mix in 1 tbsp hot water until the icing is smooth. It should be thick enough to coat the back of the spoon. Mix in colouring if used.

VARIATIONS:
CITRUS: *Replace the water with orange or lemon juice.*
ROSE: *Replace the water with rosewater.*
MOCHA: *Dissolve 1 tsp instant coffee powder in 1 tsp water. Sift 1 tsp cocoa powder with the icing sugar and mix together with the coffee, adding extra water if too thick.*
FEATHERING: *Keep a little icing separate and colour it, then place in a small piping bag. Cover the cake with plain icing and pipe parallel lines or circles of coloured icing at 2.5cm/1inch intervals. Draw a skewer through the piped lines at equal intervals in alternate directions.*

CRÈME AU BEURRE
(RICH BUTTERCREAM)

COVERS A 20CM (8") ROUND CAKE

To make this successfully you will need a sugar thermometer.

- 75 G/3 OZ CASTER SUGAR
- 2 EGG YOLKS, SIZE 3, BEATEN
- 150 G/5 OZ UNSALTED BUTTER

1 Place the sugar and 4 tbsp water in a heavy-based saucepan. Heat gently until the sugar has completely dissolved, then boil rapidly for 3–5 minutes until a temperature of 108°C/220°F is reached.

2 Pour the syrup slowly on to the yolks in a thin stream and whisk until the mixture is thick and cold.

3 Beat the butter in a separate bowl until very soft, then gradually beat in the egg yolk mixture until thick and glossy. Do not refrigerate the buttercream, but store in a cool place until needed.

VARIATIONS:
CHOCOLATE: *Gently melt 50g/2oz plain chocolate in a heatproof bowl set over warm water or in the microwave oven, then beat into the finished buttercream.*
FRUIT: *Crush 100g/4oz fresh raspberries, strawberries or apricots and beat well into the finished buttercream.*
CITRUS: *Add the finely grated zest of 1 orange, lemon or lime to the finished buttercream.*
NUT: *Stir 2 tbsp chopped nuts into the finished buttercream.*
COFFEE: *Dissolve 1 tbsp instant coffee powder in 2 tbsp boiling water and beat into the finished buttercream.*

SOFT CHEESE ICING

- 100 G/4 OZ FULL-FAT SOFT CHEESE
- 75 G/3 OZ ICING SUGAR, SIFTED
- FINELY GRATED ZEST 1 LEMON
- 2 TBSP LEMON JUICE

1 Place the cheese in a bowl with the sugar, zest and juice. Beat with a wooden spoon until soft and creamy.

CHOCOLATE FUDGE ICING

COVERS A 20CM (8") ROUND CAKE

- 100 G/4 OZ PLAIN CHOCOLATE
- 50 G/2 OZ BUTTER
- 1 EGG, SIZE 3, BEATEN
- 175 G/6 OZ ICING SUGAR, SIFTED

1 Break up the chocolate and place in a heatproof bowl with the butter. Set over a saucepan of warm water and melt gently, stirring occasionally. Beat in the egg.

2 Remove from the heat, then beat in the icing sugar until the mixture is smooth. For a smooth finish, cover the cake with warm icing; for a thicker finish, leave the icing to cool before spreading on the cake.

ITALIAN MERINGUE

COVERS A 20CM (8") ROUND CAKE

- 100 G/4 OZ CASTER SUGAR
- 2 EGG WHITES, SIZE 3

1 Heat the sugar and 6 tbsp water in a heavy-based saucepan until the sugar has completely dissolved. Bring to the boil without stirring and boil until the mixture reaches 120°C/248°F on a sugar thermometer (hard ball stage). During boiling, wash down any sugar crystals on the side of the saucepan with a pastry brush dipped in cold water.

2 Whisk the egg whites until stiff. Pour the sugar syrup slowly on to the whites, whisking at high speed, and whisk until the mixture cools. It should be stiff and glossy. Swirl over the cake with a palette knife.

SOURED CREAM CHOCOLATE ICING

COVERS A 20CM (8") ROUND CAKE

- 225 G/8 OZ PLAIN CHOCOLATE
- 300 ML/½ PINT SOURED CREAM

1 Break up the chocolate and melt very gently in a heatproof bowl set over a pan of warm water or in the microwave oven. Stir the soured cream into the melted chocolate and mix together quickly.

2 Place the cake on a wire rack set over a tray to catch the drips, then pour the icing over quickly, scooping up the drips and patching any uncovered areas. Leave to cool completely and set.

QUICK CHOCOLATE ICING

COVERS AND FILLS A 20 CM (8") ROUND CAKE

- 225 G/8 OZ SOFT TUB MARGARINE
- 4 TBSP GOLDEN SYRUP
- 8 TBSP COCOA POWDER, SIFTED

1 Place all the ingredients in a saucepan and heat gently until melted and smooth.

2 Cool the icing quickly by standing the pan in a bowl of iced water. Stir until the icing thickens, then pour immediately over the cake to cover. Leave to set.

CRÈME PÂTISSIÈRE

MAKES 300 ML / ½ PINT

- 2 EGGS, SIZE 3
- 50 G/2 OZ CASTER SUGAR, (PREFERABLY STORED WITH A VANILLA POD)
- 2 TBSP PLAIN FLOUR
- 2 TBSP CORNFLOUR
- 300 ML/½ PINT FULL-FAT MILK
- VANILLA ESSENCE (IF NECESSARY)

1 Whisk the eggs and sugar together until the mixture is pale and thick. Sift the flour and cornflour into a bowl and stir in a little milk to form a paste. Whisk into the egg mixture.

2 Heat the remaining milk until almost boiling, then pour on to the egg mixture, stirring well all the time. Return to the saucepan and stir over a low heat until boiling. Add a few drops of vanilla essence (if you are not using vanilla-flavoured sugar) and cook over a low heat, stirring constantly, until thick and smooth. Pour into a bowl and cover with dampened greaseproof paper to prevent a skin forming on the surface. Leave to cool before using.

APRICOT GLAZE

- 50 G/2 OZ APRICOT JAM

1 Place the jam and 1 tbsp water in a saucepan and heat gently to melt the jam. Bring to the boil, then simmer for 1 minute. Pass through a metal sieve. Use warm, or store in a lidded container in the refrigerator, and heat to use.

VARIATION:
REDCURRANT GLAZE: *Use redcurrant jelly instead of apricot jam and add ½ tsp lemon juice.*

AMERICAN BUTTERCREAM

FILLS AND COVERS A 20CM (8") ROUND CAKE

- 2 EGG WHITES
- 100 G/4 OZ ICING SUGAR, SIFTED

- 100 G/4 OZ UNSALTED BUTTER, AT ROOM TEMPERATURE

1 Place the egg whites in a clean, grease-free heatproof bowl. Sift in the icing sugar and set the bowl over a saucepan of hot but not boiling water.

2 Whisk until the mixture thickens and leaves a ribbon trail when the whisk is lifted. Remove the bowl from the saucepan and whisk until the mixture is cool and stands up in peaks.

3 Beat the butter until light and fluffy, then add the meringue mixture, a little at a time, beating well. Use immediately.

VARIATIONS:
CHOCOLATE: *Add 50g/2oz melted plain chocolate.*
CITRUS: *Add 1 tsp finely grated orange, lime or lemon zest and 1 tbsp juice.*

SIMPLE BUTTERCREAM

COVERS TOP AND SIDES OF A 20CM (8") CAKE

- 100 G/4 OZ UNSALTED BUTTER, AT ROOM TEMPERATURE
- 225 G/8 OZ ICING SUGAR, SIFTED

- FEW DROPS VANILLA ESSENCE OR OTHER FLAVOURING
- FOOD COLOURING (OPTIONAL)
- 1—2 TBSP WARM MILK

1 Cream the butter until very soft, using an electric mixer if possible. Beat in the sugar, a little at a time, to avoid clouds of dust. Beat in the flavourings and colouring if used, then the milk to give a good spreading consistency.

2 Use immediately or keep stored in the refrigerator or freezer until needed.

VARIATIONS:
CHOCOLATE: *Add 25g/1oz melted plain chocolate, or 2 tbsp cocoa powder dissolved in 2 tsp boiling water. Cool, then beat into basic buttercream.*
MOCHA: *Dissolve 1 tsp cocoa powder in 1 tbsp strong black coffee and add in place of the milk.*
CITRUS: *Omit the vanilla essence; replace the milk with fresh orange or lemon juice and add the finely grated zest of ½ an orange or lemon.*
LUXURY: *Replace the milk with Grand Marnier or other orange liqueur or with rum, brandy, sweet sherry, or Madeira.*

QUICK ROYAL FROSTING

COVERS A 20CM (8") ROUND CAKE

- 2 EGG WHITES, SIZE 3 EGGS
- 400 G/14 OZ ICING SUGAR, SIFTED

1 Whisk the egg whites lightly, then gradually whisk in the icing sugar until the frosting is soft and glossy. Spread on to the cake with a palette knife.

PRALINE

- 75 G/3 OZ CASTER SUGAR
- 50 G/2 OZ SHELLED ALMONDS, BLANCHED AND SKINNED

1 Oil a baking sheet. Place the sugar and 4 tbsp water in a heavy-based saucepan. Heat gently until the sugar has completely dissolved, then increase the heat until it begins to turn golden.

2 Add the nuts and quickly swirl round in the pan. Pour on to the baking sheet, spread out and leave to cool and harden.

3 Place the praline in a food processor and grind roughly, or put in a strong polythene bag and crush with a rolling pin.

PRALINE CREAM

Whip 300ml/½ pint double cream, then fold in the praline. Use to fill or decorate cakes. Alternatively, cover the cake with cream and press praline on to the sides of cake for a neat finish. Or place strips of greaseproof paper across the top of the cake and sprinkle praline across to make a stripy pattern.

CARAMEL-DIPPED ALMONDS

Whole almonds can be half or completely dipped in the caramel above and left to set separately on an oiled baking sheet. Dip them using tongs or tweezers, being careful not to get any of the boiling caramel near your hands. The French use these almonds a lot, arranged in daisy shapes on their tiered wedding cakes.

CAKE DECORATION

CHAPTER TEN

ℰ ver since nuts and sugar came to us through the trade routes, cakes have been decorated. The era of grand pâtissèrie and decoration began in France with Anton Careme. He used ground sugar in the most innovative ways, based on sculpture and architecture, and his highly elaborate designs paved the way for the cake designs we know today.

Cake decoration or sugarcraft, as it is known, has now become a widespread hobby, with many amateur local guilds producing highly skilled decorated cakes for competitions and exhibitions. The ability to produce a lavishly decorated cake for a wedding or just a simple one for tea is highly prized, and comes only by developing skills with lots of practice. This does give a great sense of achievement, so I hope you will follow some of the guidelines on the next few pages and have as much fun decorating cakes as I do.

CAKE
DECORATION

Place cakes over rolled paste

to cut exact top

Cut a long strip and wrap

round cake sides

For straight sides, cut four

separate strips

$\mathcal{A}$LMOND PASTE

To achieve a perfect finish on a decorated cake, you need a really good base to work on. Almond paste is used to seal in the cake, protecting the icing from crumbs and moisture, and also gives you the opportunity to rectify faults such as slopes, bumps or a broken cake, before you ice the cake.

Place the covered cake on a cake board 5–8cm/2–3 inches larger than the cake, to give a balanced finish and protect the sides of the cake. See pages 160–1 for recipes and quantity guide.

COVERING A CAKE WITH ALMOND PASTE

Use this method for round, square and all types of shaped cakes.

1 Remove any paper wrappings and place the cake on a flat surface. Roll with a rolling pin to flatten the surface slightly, or trim level if necessary. Brush the top of the cake with apricot glaze (see page 169).

2 Sprinkle a flat clean surface with sifted icing or caster sugar. Knead two-thirds of the measured almond paste into a ball and roll it out to 5mm/¼ inch thickness, the same shape as the top of the cake.

3 Turn the cake, glazed side down, on to the paste. Trim away the excess paste to within 1cm/½inch of the cake sides, then fold this up, pressing it to the sides to give an even edge to the top.

4 Turn the cake right way up and place on a cake board. Brush the sides with more apricot glaze. Knead the almond paste trimmings into the remaining almond paste, making sure not to include any crumbs or spots of jam. Patch any holes or gaps in the sides with small scraps of almond paste.

5 Measure a piece of string that will wrap all the way around a round cake or that is the length of one side of a square cake. Roll out the remaining paste into a strip (or four strips for a square cake), the length of the piece of string and wide enough to cover the sides.

6 Loosely roll up the paste strip into a coil. Press one end on to the cake and then unroll the paste round it, pressing it on as you go.

7 Press top and side joins together and smooth out with a palette knife. Leave the almond paste to dry out for at least 24 hours in a cool dry place, or ideally 1 week if you are planning to use royal icing. This drying is vital, as the oils from the almond paste can seep into royal icing if it is not sufficiently dried out first.

$\mathscr{R}$OYAL ICING

Royal icing is used to cover and form beautiful decorations, particularly on wedding cakes. This firm icing keeps particularly well and forms a strong seal which also preserves the flavour and texture of the cake inside. To produce these results, it is essential to make good royal icing of the right texture. (See recipe and quantity guide on pages 162–3.)

COVERING A CAKE WITH ROYAL ICING

Cover a cake with royal icing in stages – cover the top first and leave to dry out for 24 hours, then trim away any rough edges and cover the sides. Give yourself plenty of time if it is a large, tiered wedding cake. Before you start, check that the surface is level, and trim away any bumps. This is much easier to do at this stage, and it will prevent a tilting cake. Don't use royal icing until the almond paste is completely dry. Prepare the royal icing and keep the bowl covered with a damp cloth at all times; this prevents a hard skin from forming, which will break into hard lumps if stirred in.

*Work royal icing over top
and sides of cake*

TO COVER THE TOP

1 Place the cake on its board on a flat rigid surface. Place half the measured icing on top of the cake, then work it over the top using a palette knife in a spreading movement. Spread the icing until all the almond paste is covered.

2 Stand directly in front of the cake and take a steel icing ruler that is longer than the diameter of the cake. Hold the ruler at an angle of 45° and, with a firm movement, pull the ruler over the icing across the cake, towards you. Sweep the ruler back in the opposite direction, still at an angle, and continue until the top is completely smooth. Be careful not to press down too hard or the icing will become too thin.

3 Scoop away any excess icing from the sides with a palette knife to give a clean, neat edge. Leave to dry Out for 24 hours.

*Pull a steel ruler across
to smooth top*

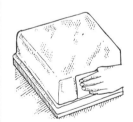

*Smooth sides with an
icing scraper*

1 This is easier to do on a turntable. If you don't have an icing turntable, stand the cake on a large-based, upturned bowl.

2 For square cakes: cover the two opposite sides first, using a small palette knife. With a plastic icing scraper, pull the icing towards you to straighten and flatten it. Trim the edges straight and leave to dry out for 24 hours, then cover the other two sides in the same way.

3 For round cakes: place the cake on a turntable and smooth the icing on the sides with a palette knife. Position your left arm as far round the cake as possible, holding the edge of the board. Hold a plastic icing scraper upright in the right hand and rotate the cake slowly in an anti-clockwise movement. Sweep the scraper round in one movement and pull it away at the point where you started. Leave to dry out. Any thin lines can be smoothed down with fine sandpaper when the icing is dry.

4 Store the cake in a cool dry place. If the storage area is too warm the oil from the almond paste may sweat into the icing, and too damp a place will not allow the icing to dry out.

THE SECOND COAT

After 24 hours, take a critical look at the outline and sides. With a sharp knife, pare away any bumps and make the surface level with fine sandpaper. Apply a second thin coat of icing and leave to dry out for 48 hours.

THE FINAL COAT

Repeat the trimming and sandpapering processes. Take a little royal icing and gently press it into any holes or gaps with a clean fingertip. Make a batch of thin icing and leave it to stand for 24 hours to allow any air bubbles to escape to the surface. Cover the cake carefully with the final coat of icing and leave to dry out, then decorate with piped decorations.

$\mathscr{F}$ONDANT ICING

Fondant paste can be rolled out and smoothed over a cake in a matter of minutes. It is also a versatile icing and can be moulded into thin dainty frills or flowers or modelled into practically any shape. (See recipe and quantity guide on pages 164–5.)

COVERING A CAKE WITH FONDANT ICING

1 Brush the marzipanned cake with sherry or boiled water so the fondant will stick.

2 Roll out the fondant icing to 5mm/¼inch thickness on a surface lightly dusted with icing sugar. Move the rolled fondant continually to prevent it from sticking. Measure the cake's circumference and sides and roll the fondant 2–5cm/1–2inches larger, to cover the whole cake.

3 Lift the fondant carefully on to the cake, holding it with both hands flat until it is in a central position, covering the whole cake.

4 Dust your hands with icing sugar and smooth the icing into position. Treat it like fabric and flute out the bottom edges, but do not pleat them as this will leave a line.

5 Very gently smooth down in one direction to remove air bubbles under the icing. Press the fondant on, and trim the edges with a sharp knife. Roll any scraps into a ball and keep tightly wrapped in a thick polythene bag.

6 If any air bubbles remain on top of the cake, prick them with a pin and smooth over. Use the flat of your hand (don't wear rings or these will leave ridges in the icing) or a special icing smoother to flatten and smooth the top, using a circular movement.

7 The cake can be decorated with a royal icing piped border, and piped or fondant decorations straightaway. Crimped patterns can be marked on to the cake, but do these immediately, before the fondant dries and becomes less pliable.

Roll icing out slightly larger than cake

Smooth icing gently around the sides

$\mathscr{F}$ONDANT FLOWERS

Roses
Roses can be made in different size and are much simpler to make than they appear.

1 Take a small coloured piece of fondant about the size of a pea. Roll it into a ball, then pull one end to a point to make a tear-drop shape. Take another pea-sized piece and flatten it out thinly to make an oval-shaped petal. If you are not sure of the shape, look at a real rose petal. Wrap the petal right round the tear-drop bud.

2 Continue to make petals, keeping the edges as thin as possible, and wrap these around the bud. As you position each petal, pinch it into the base and flute out the edges to give a natural effect.

3 Continue to add petals until the rose is the right size, then very carefully pull away the thick base, and smooth the end. Place in an old egg box lined with crumpled foil to dry out for 48 hours, in a cool dry place.

Smooth baseline with edge of a knife

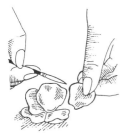

Fondant briar rose: roll icing
and cut into petals

Flute edges of each petal
with a tool

Secure petals together at base
with royal icing

Briar roses

Briar roses take longer to make, as each petal is made and dried before being assembled into a flower. These are my favourite flowers. They double up as pretty dog roses, blushed with pink petals for summer wedding cakes, or you can leave them pure white with yellow centres, for Christmas roses.

1 Roll the fondant out thinly on a surface dusted with cornflour, then cut out into petals, using a cutter, or by hand with a sharp knife.

2 Place a petal in the palm of your hand and press out the edges about two-thirds of the way round with your finger or a plastic tool, thus causing the edges to flute up and make the centre round and dipped. Place the petal on a piece of crumpled foil to support the shape and dry it out. Dry for 48 hours.

3 To assemble, pipe a small dot of royal icing on to the base of each petal, then arrange in a circle in a bun tray lined with foil. Pipe yellow dots in the centre and attach florist's stamens, if liked. Dry for 24 hours, then attach to the cake.

Daisies

1 Roll a small ball of white fondant into a tear-drop shape, then flatten out the bulbous end until thin, and pinch the long end into a stalk shape.

2 Using a small pair of clean scissors, snip tiny petals all round. Use the scissor tips to make indentations in the middle for the stamens.

3 Fluff out the petals, then leave to dry on crumpled foil for 24 hours. Using edible food colouring, paint the outer tips of the petals a very faint pink and dab the centres with a little yellow.

Carnations

1 Roll out a small ball of fondant on a surface lightly dusted with cornflour. Cut out a small round with a small fluted pastry cutter. Make 5mm/¼inch deep cuts round the outer edge, then make smaller slashes between the deep cuts. This gives the jagged edge.

2 Roll a wooden cocktail stick backwards and forwards around each curve until the edge flutes and frills up. Continue with the next curve until all the edge is frilled.

3 Carefully fold the round in half, then in half again. Make four petals like this. Pinch three together in a bunch, then wrap the fourth one round the outside to enclose them. Fluff out the edges with the tip of a cocktail stick, then leave in an egg box lined with foil to dry out for 48 hours.

Blossom

1 Roll a small ball of white fondant into a cone shape, then hollow this out over the top of a clean ball point pen top, or similar shape.

2 Cut five tiny petals with nail scissors, then flatten and pinch each petal together with your fingers.

3 Pipe a yellow dot in the centre or attach florist's stamens. Dry out for 24 hours, then use arranged in small bunches.

Leaves

1 On a surface lightly sprinkled with cornflour, thinly roll out some green-coloured fondant. Cut out oval shapes with a cutter or sharp knife.

2 With the point of a sharp knife, mark on the central and side veins, then twist the end of each leaf. Leave to dry out on foil for 24 hours.

Fondant daisy: make a hollow cone from a ball

Snip all around the cone nearly to the base

Fondant rose: wrap a petal shape around a teardrop bud

Pinch base of each petal on to base of bud

Continue to wrap petals around bud

Pull away the excess base, and smooth

Bend the strips back, and thread through a wired fondant core

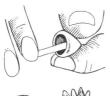

Fondant blossom: hollow out a small cone, then snip round and pinch into points

Thread through a florist's stamen

*Curl one corner into the
middle of the triangle*

*Pull the bottom corner round
to make a cone*

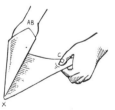

*Pull to tighten and make
a sharp point*

*Wrap corner round and fold
over top to secure*

$\mathscr{P}$IPING

Royal icing, buttercream and crème au beurre can all be piped on to cakes to decorate them. The art of piping requires a steady hand, and lots of practice. Ordinary buttercream can be used for practising on a clean table-top or cake boards.

Most decoration can be achieved with simple nozzles fitted into non-stick silicone paper or greaseproof paper bags, so just invest in a few basic ones. A plain writing nozzle and small and large star nozzles will get you started.

The icing used for piping must be smooth and completely free of lumps, or these will block the nozzle. It must be soft enough to force through the nozzle, but firm enough to hold its shape.

Making a paper piping bag

There are many plastic piping bags on the market with nozzles and connecting bolts. These are useful if you have a lot of piping to do with the same colour, but I prefer to make small paper piping bags for each colour. These are also easier to handle as you can get a good grip on them, using the strength of your palm to force out the icing, and not your arm muscles. If you do lots of icing over a few hours, your arm will start to ache if you are not comfortable, so don't grapple with large over-filled bags.

Always use the strongest paper you can buy. Non-stick silicone paper is stronger than greaseproof; if only greaseproof is available, then use it double thickness. There is nothing more infuriating than a bag which splits halfway through its use.

1 Cut out a 25cm/10inch square, then cut in half diagonally to make a triangle.

2 Keeping the longest edge in front of you, take a corner point and curl it into the middle (A). Curl the other corner to the middle and wrap round to form a cone with a sharp point (B).

3 Secure the top by folding the top edge over twice.

Filling a paper piping bag

Half fill the bag only. If you add more icing the bag will split or burst and you will end up in a mess! Fold the top edge down until the bag is sealed and firm, then fold over again to seal it. Hold the bag across the palm of one hand, place your thumb over the top, then grasp the fingers round the bag. Apply even pressure to force the icing out of the bag.

Stars

Fit a star nozzle into the bag. Hold the bag upright above the surface of the cake and squeeze out the icing. When the star appears, stop pressing and lift the bag away.

Shells

Use a star or special shell nozzle. Hold the bag at a 45° angle, just touching the cake. Press out the icing until a rounded shape forms. Release the pressure and gently pull the nozzle away, pulling the tail downwards on to the cake. Make the next shell 5mm/¼inch away from the first. Press out the icing; as it makes the rounded shape it should meet the tail of the preceeding shell.

Scrolls

Use a star nozzle. Hold the bag at a 90° angle to the cake. Press out the icing to make a shell shape, but twist the nozzle in a circular shape like the tail of an 'S'. Pull the bag away to make a tail, then pipe the next scroll to meet this tail.

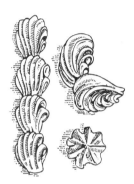

Dots

Use a plain nozzle or snip a small hole in the end of the paper bag. Place the tip of the nozzle on the surface and hold the bag upright. Squeeze the bag gently, at the same time lifting it away. Only slight pressure is required. Move the nozzle away, using no pressure, or you will get a 'tail'. Larger dots can be made by moving the nozzle in a small circle.

Piped stars and shells

Straight lines

Place the tip of the nozzle where the line is to begin. Press the bag and as the icing starts to come out, lift it away from the surface. Guide the bag in the direction of the line. Before the end of the line stop squeezing and lower the nozzle down on to the surface to finish.

Writing

Use a small plain nozzle. Follow the technique above, guiding the string of icing into place. Practise on a plate first, to ensure that all the letters will fit in. Draw the letters on greaseproof paper and prick them through to the cake with a pin as a guide for total precision.

Piped lettering

$\mathcal{C}$HOCOLATE
DECORATIONS

Chocolate curls, *caraque* and leaves can add that final touch to a cake. They are easy to make, but give yourself plenty of time to allow the chocolate to cool and set.

Chocolate curls

Using a potato peeler, scrape off curls from a block of chocolate. This will work better if the chocolate is at room temperature as the curls come away easily in one piece.

Chocolate caraque

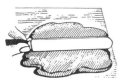

Pour melted chocolate over a work surface

1 Melt the chocolate gently in a heatproof bowl set over a pan of warm water. Spread it out on a marble slab or clean cool work surface, spreading from side to side with a palette knife to make a large flat pool. Leave to cool and set.

Spread out with a palette knife

2 When set, scrape off large curls using a large sharp knife held at both ends, pulling it slowly towards you over the chocolate. Refrigerate curls until needed.

Chocolate leaves

Wash and dry rose leaves, then brush the back of the leaf with a thin layer of melted chocolate. Drape over the handle of a wooden spoon to dry, then carefully peel away the leaves when the chocolate is set.

Scrape chocolate curls with a potato peeler

Scrape off long curls with a sharp knife

184

$\mathcal{S}$UGAR-FROSTED
FLOWERS, FRUITS
AND LEAVES

*Frosted flowers and fruits add an attractive finish to a cake and are
simple to make. They keep well for up to 2 weeks in an airtight
container between layers of tissue. Some flowers will keep longer
than this, but fruits will not.*

FRUIT, FLOWERS OR LEAVES OF CHOICE (SEE BELOW)	1 EGG WHITE CASTER SUGAR

*Brush flowers or fruits
with whisked egg white*

1 Make sure the fruit, flowers or leaves are clean and completely dry. Place the egg white in a small bowl and whisk with 2 tsp water until lightly frothy.

2 Dip or paint the flower with the egg white, until evenly coated, then sprinkle or roll in caster sugar. Leave to dry on non-stick silicone paper that has been lightly dusted with caster sugar.

3 Use to decorate large or small cakes, when the icing is still wet.

FLOWERS: *Choose flowers with a few petals only, or divide large flowers like roses into separate petals. Small flowers like primroses and violets are ideal, but never use narcissi, as these contain a poison.*
FRUITS: *Small fruits and currants work best; choose red or black currants, grapes, cherries or segmented mandarin oranges.*
LEAVES: *These should be small, and the leaves of herbs like mint, bay or rosemary look particularly pretty.*

'Any Number' of Cakes

I've often been asked to make cakes in the shape of a number, especially for children's birthday parties. These can present problems as the tins are very expensive to buy or hire, and you really don't know how much mixture they will hold or how long the cakes will take to bake. I always take the easy way, and stick to a tried and trusted recipe, baked in an 18cm/7inch square tin or a 23cm/9inch flat-based ring tin. There is a bit of chopping and sticking back together involved, but I find this method produces good results, with very little waste. If there are any spare pieces over, freeze them away for making trifles, or chocolate truffles.

NUMBER 1

Bake a square cake. Simply cut down the centre, position on a board and stick the two short ends together with jam.

NUMBER 2

Bake one square cake and one ring cake. Cut as shown in the diagram. Remove the curved cut third from the ring, and turn it round in the opposite direction to make a question mark shape. Cut a long oblong and a short square from the square cake and position them along the base. Seal all the joins with jam.

NUMBER 3

Bake two ring cakes and cut as shown in the diagram. Place the one with the largest section cut out at the base and the other one adjoining it. Seal the join with jam.

NUMBER 4

Bake two square cakes, and cut down the centre as shown. Remove a small section from one block as shown on the diagram, then position the oblongs on a board, sealing all the joins with jam.

NUMBER 5

Bake one square cake and one ring cake, and cut as shown. Position the two oblongs to form a right angle, then stick the curved base piece in place.

NUMBER 6 AND NUMBER 9

Bake one square cake and one ring cake, and cut as shown. Position and stick the two oblongs together, then place the curved piece at the base, and stick with jam. For Number 9, simply use the same cakes but position upside-down.

NUMBER 7

Bake two square cakes and cut as shown. Stick the two sets of oblongs together at a slanting angle, and secure with jam.

NUMBER 8

Bake two ring cakes and trim the tops as shown. Position and join the two rings together on a board.

NUMBER 0

Bake one square cake and one ring cake. Cut the ring in half and cut two oblongs as shown. Position and stick the two semi-circles at either end of the oblongs.

TIN TIP

If you don't own a ring tin, then use a 23cm/9inch round deep cake tin and place a 7.5cm/3inch wide empty fruit or baked bean tin in the centre. Grease and line the outside of the fruit or bean tin, then fill with weights or baking beans, to prevent it moving around during baking.

Illustrated opposite page 161

*Create numerals with cut
sponge lengths as shown*

$\mathcal{S}$ UPPLIERS

Ingredients for making cakes and pastries can be found from most supermarkets and grocers but for obtaining specialist decoration supplies the following list might be helpful:

UNITED KINGDOM

THE BRITISH SUGARCRAFT GUILD
Wellington House, Messeter Place, Eltham, London SE9 5DP.

CAKE ART LTD
Wholesale suppliers of icings and equipment. Unit 16, Crown Close, Crown Industrial Estate, Priors Wood, Taunton, Somerset TA2 8RX.

COVENT GARDEN KITCHEN SUPPLIES
3 North Row, The Market, Covent Garden, London WC2 8RA.

CRAFT CENTRES
360 Leach Place, Bamber Bridge, Preston, Lancashire PR5 8AR.

CREATING CAKES
The Mall, 123 East Street, Sittingbourne, Kent ME10 4BL

CYNTHIA VENN
3 Anker Lane, Stubbington, Fareham, Hants PO14 3HF.

GUY PAUL & CO. LTD
Unit 81, A1 Industrial Park, Little End Road, Eaton Socon, Cambridgeshire PE19 3JH.

HOMEBAKERS SUPPLIES
157–159 High Street, Wolstanton, Newcastle, Staffs ST5 0EJ.

HOUSE OF CAKES
18 Meadow Close, Woodley, Stockport, Cheshire SK6 1QZ.

JENNY CAMPBELL/B.R.
MATTHEWS & SON
12 Gypsy Hill, Upper Norwood, London SE19 1NN.

JF RENSHAW LTD
Suppliers of icings. Locks Lane, Mitcham, Surrey CR4 2XG.

KITCHENS
167 Whiteladies Road, Bristol, Avon BS8 2SQ *and*
4–5 Quiet Street, Bath, BA1 2JS.

KNIGHTSBRIDGE BUSINESS CENTRE
(WILTON UK)
Knightsbridge, Cheltenham, Gloucestershire GL51 9TA.

LINCOLN HOUSE
Cake Decorating Centre, 198 Desborough Road, High Wycombe, Bucks HP11 2QA.

MARY FORD CAKE ARTISTRY
CENTRE LTD
28–30 Southbourne Grove, Southbourne, Bournemouth, Dorset BH6 3RA.

MIDLANDS ICING CENTRE
10 Moat Lane, Great Wyrley, Nr Walsall, West Midlands WS6 6DU.

PHOENIX KITCHEN
349 Ballards Lane, Tally Ho Corner, Finchley, London N12 8LJ.

A PIECE OF CAKE
18 Upper High Street, Thames, Oxon OX9 3EX.

QUALITY CAKES
1 Grassmere Parade, Felpham , Bognor Regis, West Sussex PO22 7NT.

RAINBOW RIBBONS
Unit D5, Romford Seedbed Centre, Davidson Way, Romford, Essex RM7 0AZ.

SARAH WATERKEYN
29 Lambs Conduit Street, London WC1N 3NG.

SPECIALITY SUGARCRAFT PRODUCTS
143 Quebec Road, Blackburn, Lancs BB2 7DP.

AUSTRALIA

AUSTRALIAN NATIONAL CAKE
DECORATORS' ASSOCIATION
PO Box 321, Plympton, SA 5038.

CAKE DECORATING ASSOCIATION
OF VICTORIA
President, Shirley Vaas, 4 Northcote Road, Ocean Grove, Victoria 3226.

CAKE DECORATING GUILD OF
NEW SOUTH WALES
President, Fay Gardiner, 4 Horsley Cres, Melba, Act, 2615.

NEW ZEALAND

NEW ZEALAND CAKE DECORATORS
GUILD
Secretary, Morag Scott, 17 Ranui Terrace, Tawa, Wellington.

DECOR CAKES
RSA Arcade, 435 Great South Road, Otahaha.

SOUTH AFRICA

SOUTH AFRICAN SUGARCRAFT GUILD
National Office, 1 Tuzla Mews, 187 Smit Street, Fairlan 2195.

$\mathcal{I}$NDEX